T0112939

SERVICE DOG
TRAINING GUIDE

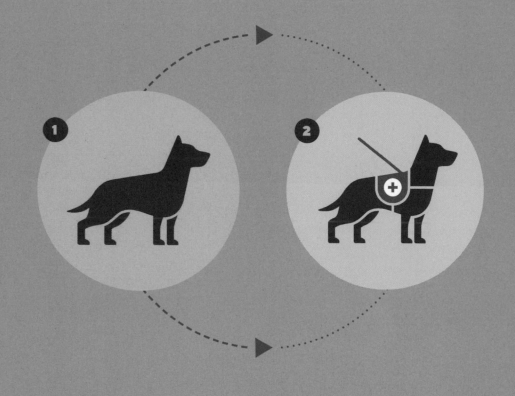

SERVICE DOG TRAINING GUIDE

A STEP-BY-STEP TRAINING PROGRAM FOR YOU AND YOUR DOG

JENNIFER HACK

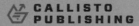

CALLISTO PUBLISHING

Copyright © 2020 by Callisto Publishing LLC
Cover and internal design © 2020 by Callisto Publishing LLC
Custom Illustrations © 2020 Kate Francis
Interior art used under license from © Shutterstock.com
Art Director: Liz Cosgrove
Art Producer: Michael Hardgrove
Editor: Arturo Conde
Production Editor: Andrew Yackira

Published by Callisto Publishing LLC C/O Sourcebooks LLC
P.O. Box 4410, Naperville, Illinois 60567-4410
(630) 961-3900
callistopublishing.com

Printed and bound in China.
OGP 24

This book is dedicated to those living with different abilities and their canine partners.

CONTENTS

What Can a
Service Dog
Do for Me?

viii

ONE
Identifying and
Understanding
Service Dogs

2

TWO
Rules and
Training for Your
Service Dog

20

THREE
General Service
Dog Tasks

42

FOUR
Psychiatric
and Medical
Assistance Tasks

82

FIVE

Mobility
Support Tasks

110

SIX

How to Get
Your Service
Dog Certified

134

Resources

143

Index

146

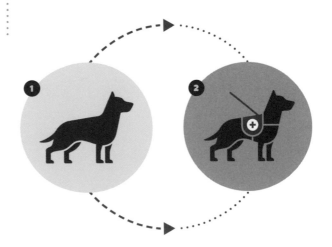

WHAT CAN A SERVICE DOG DO FOR ME?

SERVICE DOGS are highly trained animals that assist people living with physical and psychiatric disabilities. Because they can perform day-to-day tasks and activities that are essential to their owner's safety and health, service dogs can be life-changing, enhancing both independence and quality of life.

Dogs have been assisting humans with specific tasks for thousands of years. According to historians, the oldest record of such behavior dates back to the first century AD—a fresco in the ancient Roman city Herculaneum shows a blind man being led by his dog. The modern guide dog movement started in post–World War I Germany to assist soldiers who were visually impaired during combat. Since then, we have developed ways to train service dogs that can assist those living with any number of disabilities and conditions by performing a variety of essential tasks.

This book is for people who want to learn practical ways to task train their own service dog and covers how dogs learn, how to teach tasks, and tips and tricks to help you along the way. The guide is intended to complement your training pro-gram. Basic to advanced obedience is a major part of training a service dog, so it's important to use this book in conjunction with an obedience training program. If you are raising a puppy as a service dog prospect, it's also vital to read up on puppy socialization and training (see Resources on page 143).

It's important to note that having a diagnosis does not automatically qualify someone for a service dog. The condition must be substantially limiting for one or more major life activi-ties, and this is highly individual. It is up to you to determine what will work best for you—there is, of course, no "one way" to live with disabilities.

The benefits of owning a service dog can be great, but before committing to one, carefully examine the cons as well, includ-ing the financial and time commitments. Although this book frequently offers cost-saving suggestions, all dogs need sup-plies, grooming, and veterinary care. They also depend on humans for day-to-day care, exercise, and continual training. Service dogs may also spark (wrongful) public access issues—such as unwanted attention and breaches of rights granted by the Americans with Disabilities Act (ADA)—as they typically travel everywhere with their handlers.

The road to service dog training can be long, up to two years. Just like disabilities vary greatly, the training process can also vary. You will learn to adapt the training to your needs and abilities. The first step? Believing you can do it. A positive attitude helps build your dog's desire to work, setting you up to succeed with the exercises in this book.

Progress isn't always in a straight line, and there may be challenges and setbacks along the way. Don't worry, it's not a race. It's a slow and steady investment. Take your time with each step. You will need practice to gain skills as a trainer, and your dog will need lots of repetition and reward before moving on to the next step. Your committed effort to this journey will result in a life-changing experience and an amazing partner-ship lasting many years.

TRAINING A PUPPY

Finding the right puppy for your service dog needs is crucial for training. People hire a real estate agent to help them find a house. They hire a mechanic to look over a car. But many don't consider hiring a dog trainer or behaviorist to help them find and select a puppy. And depending on the breed, your cute puppy may not be suited for service tasks that you need or want them to perform.

When looking for a puppy, patience is a virtue. Most quality breeders don't have puppies available 365 days a year—litters are planned ahead. If you come across a reputable breeder, don't hesitate to reach out to them even if they don't have puppies available. They may have a referral for you. Expect to take your time to learn about the breed, talk with breeders and trainers, and wait for your puppy to be ready to go home. Puppies should never go home before eight weeks of age. Some breeders prefer pups to go home around 10 to 12 weeks of age.

Once you have your pup, patience remains key in raising and training. Your pup has to mature before they can be considered a service dog in training. At a young age, we call them "service dog prospects." We are raising them with that goal in mind, but don't worry about starting task training right away. When you research and learn how to properly raise a pet puppy, much of it will overlap with raising a puppy as a service dog.

Puppies need structure and management. They also need time to experience puppyhood, play, and build confidence. A service dog prospect should be socialized to people, just as any puppy should be. However, greetings should only occur when allowed, not with every single person you encounter, and only when the puppy is fairly calm and under control. Overstimulation can lead to bad manners. Practice luring your puppy back to you with a treat and the cue of their name.

We want our puppy to bond with us, but we also want them to have a sense of self-confidence that allows them to handle being away from us without showing signs of stress or anxiety. In this sense, it's good for them to have some time away from your side too. These training tips will help them find the right balance:

1. Crate training is a good skill for all dogs, especially puppies. The crate serves as a safe place for short-term confinement and safe car travel, and assists with housebreaking. The crate is a place of rest, like a den. Dogs have the instinct not to potty in their confined sleeping area. Housebreaking is the shaping of that habit. Service dog prospects will also learn to potty on cue.

2. Along with a crate of the proper size, baby gates or an exercise pen (also called an "x-pen") is helpful for managing a new puppy. Any time your puppy cannot be directly supervised, they should be confined to a puppy-proof area. This is for their own safety, as well as to discourage any bad habits. A puppy should not sleep in a human's bed overnight. It can lead to overattachment. A crate in the bedroom is best.

3. Many new puppy owners are concerned about exposing their dog to the outdoors when they have not completed their vaccination series. This is something to discuss early on with your own veterinarian. However, it's detrimental for a puppy to be confined indoors until 17 weeks, as critical socialization periods would be missed. Many vets agree that the benefits of early socialization outweigh the risks of taking your puppy outside or to training classes before being fully vaccinated. Check with your vet, and consider carefully where you bring your puppy. Avoid dog parks and places where sick or unvaccinated animals may have been.

4. Beware of burnout. Sometimes the eagerness to get a puppy trained and socialized can lead to overdoing it. It's not necessary to take a young puppy with you everywhere you go. There are a lot of puppy training exercises you can do at home, including introducing marker training. Outings should be planned for times you can focus on your puppy, and kept brief for young pups under six months who are not reliably housebroken yet.

A puppy outing can include exposing them to new things and allowing them to observe and take in the environment around them at their own pace. It may also include a brief training session. Once that's accomplished, a pup may need a break or crate rest.

5. When planning visits, choose places that:

- Have an easy way out, in case you need a potty break.
- Minimize the risk of negative dog-dog interactions.
- Are not too busy, crowded, or loud for the stage your puppy is at.

Never force your puppy into situations. If they show hesitance, start from farther away next time, and remain calm and encouraging.

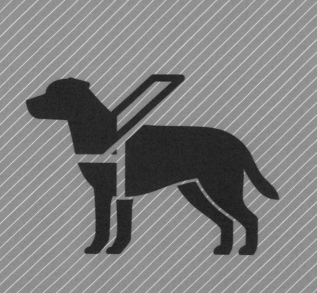

SERVICE DOG TRAINING GUIDE

ONE
IDENTIFYING AND UNDERSTANDING SERVICE DOGS

THIS CHAPTER explores what you need to know before you commit to training your dog as a service dog. A service dog is more than a pet: They are valuable pieces of medical equipment. They perform a variety of tasks aimed at helping people in different ways. However, not all dogs that help people are considered service dogs. A service dog, sometimes called an assistance dog, is one that is trained to perform specific tasks related to a disability. They also have public access rights, which means they have the right to go where other animals are forbidden.

4 KEY DIFFERENCES BETWEEN SERVICE DOGS AND OTHER DOGS

5 WHAT ARE THE DIFFERENT TYPES OF SERVICE DOGS?

7 WHAT ARE THE MOST POPULAR SERVICE DOG BREEDS?

9 SHOP OR ADOPT?

11 WHAT YOU SHOULD KNOW BEFORE TRAINING YOUR DOG

13 SHOULD YOU TRAIN AN EMOTIONAL SUPPORT DOG INSTEAD?

14 PICKING THE BEST EQUIPMENT FOR YOUR SERVICE DOG

A service dog should not be confused with other types of canine helpers. Emotional support animals (ESAs), for example, provide comfort to their handlers by their presence. However, no special training or tasks are required of them. ESAs have housing exemptions and may travel on airlines, but they do not have public access rights like service dogs do. A therapy dog is similar to an ESA, but rather than assisting an individual, a therapy dog provides comfort to many people. Calm and social, therapy dogs are often invited to visit nursing homes or hospitals but do not have public access rights.

KEY DIFFERENCES BETWEEN SERVICE DOGS AND OTHER DOGS

It takes a special dog to become a service dog. Candidates are chosen for their stable temperament and their ability and willingness to work for a person. They receive more specialized and advanced training than the average pet.

Service dog training consists of three main parts: obedience training, public access training, and specific task training. Obedience training, the foundation of a service dog's training, consists of commands such as heel, sit, down, stay, and come when called. These skills are continually developed and perfected. Obedience introduces the dog to the fun of the learning process and teaches them that you, the handler, are in charge. Reliable obedience skills also prepare the dog for smooth public access training.

Public access training involves all the appropriate skills and socialization to function in public places, including places where other animals are forbidden. A service dog experiences a variety of day-to-day situations, and they must be prepared to handle each one. This is accomplished by thoughtful exposure to new places and things during the training process. Service dogs are expected to behave in public. They can often be identified by their calm, unobtrusive behavior and their focus on their human handler. Notably, service dogs should never be out of control, disruptive, or display aggression. They are also expected to be housebroken before beginning public access training. If a puppy is too young to be reliably housebroken, it's best to keep outings short but frequent and stick to visiting places that allow pets. Service dogs in training (SDiT), who are just beginning to be exposed to working in public, start by visiting pet-friendly places such as parks, outdoor malls, and some of the large home improvement stores that allow pets. As training progresses, planned public outings provide new training opportunities. For more information on obedience and public access training, see chapter 6 (page 134).

Task training, what this book is all about, involves training the dog to perform often complex skills or jobs that help people living with specific disabilities. For example, a service dog may assist a person with limited mobility with clothing removal (see page 72), remind a person to take their medication (see page 88), or retrieve dropped items (see page 104), among many other tasks.

Service animals are not required by law to wear identification but you can often spot them by the focus and attention they give to their handlers. The best way to respond to seeing a service dog in public is to ignore it. You wouldn't go up to someone and ask to pet their wheelchair, so it's best to show respect for service dogs by not interrupting them while they're working.

Some handlers may choose to let you pet their dog if you ask, but this should never be assumed. If a handler does not want you to pet their dog, they may offer a polite and simple response: "Sorry, no, they're a service dog, and they're working." Service dogs, especially those who are in training, should not be offered treats by strangers, nor should they be distracted by other dogs in public. Having a bad encounter with another dog who isn't under control can set back their training.

WHAT ARE THE DIFFERENT TYPES OF SERVICE DOGS?

Perhaps the most frequently recognized types of service dogs are those who assist a person who is blind or someone who uses a wheelchair. The truth is that not all disabilities are visible, and service dogs are trained to assist all types of handlers and help them live safer, fuller, more independent lives. It's all about teamwork. Here's a rundown of some common types of service dogs:

Guide: Guide dogs assist those living with vision impairment or blindness. An intensive training process teaches them to work along with their handler to avoid obstacles and safely navigate the world. It's tricky to train a full-fledged "seeing eye" dog, so it's recommended that this type of training be left to the professionals. As such, this book does not cover this complex topic. Still, those living with certain disabilities or conditions may benefit from a few guide-related tasks, such as stopping for changes in elevation such as curbs, leading a person forward on cue, leading to an exit, and finding the counter in a store.

Hearing: For individuals living with hearing loss, a dog can alert them to everyday sounds, as well as emergency sounds, such as fire alarms. A hearing dog may be trained to alert their handler to a ringing phone, a doorbell, a calling child, or even a whistling kettle on the stove. Rather than barking to alert, which may go unheard or be a nuisance, they're often trained to do a nose-touch alert. They can also retrieve unheard dropped objects, such as keys.

Medical Alert and Response: There are several types of medical alert and response dogs. Diabetes alert dogs are trained to detect the scent and chemical changes of high or low blood sugar, alerting the handler before it becomes an emergency. Other tasks include fetching a medication bag or a phone. Allergen detection dogs are trained to help those with severe reactions to avoid specific substances, such as peanuts. Seizure alert dogs are a bit different, as they typically begin alerting naturally, and the behavior is then shaped. Besides alerting to an oncoming medical event, a response dog may also be trained to respond to an event once it occurs.

Mobility: These dogs are trained to assist those living with physical conditions that involve limited mobility. They may retrieve items, open and close doors and cabinets, turn lights on and off, and help with daily personal tasks. Many tasks are variations on foundational skills, such as retrieve, pull, and touch/push with nose or paw. For example, to open doors, the dog is taught to pull a rope or handle attached to the door. Some mobility dogs perform tasks for a handler who uses a wheelchair. Others may help brace a handler with balance or stability challenges.

Psychiatric: Psychiatric service dogs are trained to perform tasks related to a psychiatric or developmental disability, and they may overlap with medical response. Some psych tasks include (but are not limited to) interrupting self-harm or OCD rituals, turning on lights, grounding during panic attacks, and reminding handlers to take medications. Psych service dogs are not the same as an emotional support dog, as they perform trained tasks rather than simply comforting by their presence alone. They directly help their handler remain safe and function in their daily lives.

WHAT ARE THE MOST POPULAR SERVICE DOG BREEDS?

The Americans with Disabilities Act (ADA) allows for any breed of dog to be a service dog, but that doesn't mean every breed is as likely to succeed in this role. Much time, emotion, and work are invested in a service dog prospect. Starting with the right dog is crucial to future success.

There is a common myth that says a service dog's potential for success is "all in how you raise them." In truth, while environment and training do matter, a dog's temperament and abilities are also determined in part by their genetics.

Different types of dogs excel at different things. Many generations of selective breeding have given greyhounds the ability to chase prey with incredible speed. They are also popular pets for their likable personalities. But you wouldn't choose a greyhound to herd sheep on a farm or join the local police K9 unit. Regardless of how much training they receive, some dogs are better suited to particular jobs.

When choosing a breed to train, you can use the table below to weigh your best options.

DESIRED TRAITS	CAPABILITIES	TRAITS TO AVOID	SECONDARY PREFERENCES
tolerant	retrieve objects	nervous	appearance
stable	pull doors open	fearful	
handler-oriented	brace	suspicious of strangers	
easy to motivate	psych support	intolerant of other animals	
physically sound structure	scent detection	noise sensitive	

Consider the handler's personality. If a person frequently experiences strong emotions like anxiety or fear, those emotions can transfer over to a more sensitive dog. This can result in the dog displaying anxiety and undesirable behaviors. They may do better with a dog who is calm and even-keeled. Also consider the lifestyle and activity level of the dog.

Service dogs come in all sizes. The ideal size and weight of a service dog depends on the tasks the dog is expected to perform. A smaller dog isn't likely to retrieve heavy objects, but may do well with medical alert or psych tasks. Certain breeds of dogs are more suitable for weight-bearing mobility. The most suitable dogs are large or extra-large, square (as tall as they are long), and sturdily built. A good example is a Great Dane. Fine-boned dogs, such as sighthounds, have too flexible a spine and aren't suitable for certain types of mobility tasks. If you are seeking a giant breed puppy, keep in mind the longer growth period. Exercise or weight-bearing activities should be avoided until a dog is fully grown and cleared by a vet. Giant breeds can also have shorter working life spans.

Once you have narrowed down traits and abilities, the next step is to research each breed. Remember that intelligence does not always equal trainability. Modern breeds designed to work

SHOP OR ADOPT?

Although it's fairly easy to find a nice pet in a shelter, adopting a service dog candidate can be trickier. The reality is, only a small percentage of dogs have what it takes to become a service dog. The highest chances of finding the most predictable temperament qualities and health is by seeking a purebred through a reputable breeder—ideally, one who has a track record of success and has produced puppies that went on to become working service dogs. Do your homework on what to look for in a breeder. Start by finding the breed club. For example, if you want to learn more about labs, look up the Labrador Retriever Club of America. Breed club websites often list the recommended genetic health testing and standards a breeder should abide by. Avoid pet stores and backyard breeders who do not follow the standards of responsible breeding.

You might also choose to explore the option of obtaining your dog through a shelter or rescue. Take your time to find the right fit while keeping in mind your requirements. Find a reputable organization that assesses the temperaments of their adoptable dogs. It may be beneficial to work with a rescue that houses dogs in foster homes, as they might have more insight on the dog's personality. Evaluating a young adult dog is more accurate than evaluating a young puppy, as it's not always possible to predict how a puppy will mature, especially if its background and health are unknown.

alongside humans are often the most trainable. In contrast, dogs bred to work independently, such as livestock guardian breeds or primitive breeds, tend to be very intelligent but are generally less suited to service dog work. A husky or hound dog, for example, may have an independent attitude and require more patience to train. Similarly, some guardian breeds might not do well as service dogs due to their instinctively protective nature. If a handler has a medical episode or falls, a protective dog may become a risk to medical responders trying to help the person.

The three most common breeds for service work are Labrador retrievers, golden retrievers, and standard poodles. However, here are some additional breeds to consider:

- **Mixed breeds**

- **Smooth collie**

- **Miniature poodle**

- **Papillon**

- **German shepherd**

- **Bernese mountain dog**

- **Greater Swiss mountain dog**

- **Vizsla**

- **Flat-coated retriever**

- **German shorthaired pointer**

Just because a breed is not listed doesn't mean it can't be a service dog. There are hundreds of breeds and unique individuals within each. But these are the most tried and true. The next step is to find a dog through a reputable breeder, shelter, or rescue.

WHAT YOU SHOULD KNOW BEFORE TRAINING YOUR DOG

As discussed, task training is only part of a service dog's education. Before you can even begin task training, your dog must have a solid foundation of advanced obedience skills, such as "heel," "sit," "stay," and "come." This not only makes task training easier; it also provides the dog with the skills they need to be functional as a service dog, particularly in public spaces where the standard for behavior is very high. Chapter 2 (see page 20) includes recommended obedience skills your dog should master before task training. If your dog struggles with these basic skills, it may be an indication that they are not suited for the rigors of service dog training.

Before task training, it's important to understand how your dog learns. Dogs are naturally inclined to be aware of and respond to our body language. But how well do we know theirs? It's worth taking the time to research and study dog body language before training begins, as you'll be better able to gauge your dog's reactions and better suited to understand what they are thinking and feeling at any moment.

What motivates your dog? These answers will become the things you use as rewards. For most dogs, interaction and praise are motivating, but working for food rewards can really speed up the learning process. Some also enjoy a toy or play. The more you can get your dog to play with you, the better your relationship and training bond will be. Training tasks require a good deal of motivation.

Take a look at your dog's strengths and weaknesses. The one word that best describes the ideal temperament for a service dog is "bombproof." This means a dog is confident, calm, and able to handle many different scenarios while remaining unbothered. Can you identify any areas where your dog lacks confidence? If your dog is a mature adult, you must decide whether or not their weaknesses can easily be improved. If not, those weaknesses will interfere with their ability to perform as a service dog.

There are two phases to training: teaching and proofing. These should be applied to every exercise and task in this book. In the teaching phase, the dog receives a lot of help and guidance, especially in the beginning. For example, if you are teaching the command "down," you may guide the dog into position with gentle downward pressure on the leash, guiding them into the right position. You may also use a lure, such as a treat, to help show them what you want them to do. Next, the action is paired with a verbal command or cue. This is where tons of repetition and reward needs to happen. Use praise when the dog shows effort—and even bigger praise when the dog gets it right.

The proofing phase is when the "three Ds" of service dog training—distance, duration, and distraction—come into play. A dog is ready for the proofing phase when they can demonstrate that they clearly understand what is being asked of them by successfully completing a task 80 percent of the time (eight out of 10 attempts). In this phase, the dog learns that every command should be followed through on—no matter where they are or what is happening around them. In order for a dog to reliably listen, skills need to be consistently practiced and proofed through the three Ds.

Let's use the command "sit" as an example. When proofing for distance, you and your dog will practice "sit" as you cue from farther and farther away and from different positions, such as at the left side or "heel" position. When proofing for duration, practice cuing "sit" for increasing lengths of time, working toward a reasonable goal, such as a two- or three-minute stay. When proofing for distraction, practice cuing "sit" under mild, moderate, and high distraction, such as in public places with more people, animals, or noise.

Now that you have a basic understanding of how your dog learns, there are a few things you can do to ensure they have the best chance possible to succeed. First, always end a training session with play. Think about when you were a kid: After you did your homework, you could go out and play. The work comes first, and the play is a chance to blow off steam and have some fun. Interactive play is one of the best relationship-building activities you can do with your dog.

Next, be sure to limit indulgence and over-petting. It's tough to train a dog using food rewards if the dog gets unlimited

SHOULD YOU TRAIN AN EMOTIONAL SUPPORT DOG INSTEAD?

Some people may decide they don't need their dog with them all the time or don't need them to have public access. They might still want to train tasks for use at home. Or maybe their current dog is either not ready or not suitable to be a full-fledged service dog in public. Some dogs may be wonderful at home but have issues outside, or simply are not suited for public space. This doesn't mean your dog can't provide assistance at home. Your dog may be better suited to be an emotional support animal instead, which does not require specific skills. If this is the case, you can still use many of the service dog tasks and exercises in this book to help you train your dog for home-based assistance. Emotional support dogs do not have public access rights, but they can travel on planes and have special housing rights through HUD.

free-feeding all day. Similarly, constant affection can lower a dog's motivation to interact during the training process. Try to reserve some of your praise and enthusiastic attention for training sessions, as it will mean even more to your dog when it's earned.

Keep a training log to track progress and give you perspective. This way you can compare where your dog was at a week ago or six months ago without having to remember everything. Your training log can be as detailed as you'd like. You can use any word processor to create a training form, punch it out, and put it in a binder. Or you can log your training electronically so it's easier to organize. At a minimum, you'll want to jot down the date and a few notes on what you did with your dog.

PICKING THE BEST EQUIPMENT FOR YOUR SERVICE DOG

In addition to all the common things you'd need for any dog, there are some specific pieces of equipment that will come in handy when training and living with your service dog.

First, a roll-up or easily carried travel mat is useful to place as a resting spot. Service dogs tend to spend a lot of time lying down or tucked under a chair calmly resting. Having their own mat can be preferable to lying on a hard floor. It can also protect your dog from the dirt and grime on the floors in public spaces, such as a movie theater. In the beginning, you can train your dog to lie down anytime you lay the mat out.

Which training tools work best for your dog depends on many factors, including their age, size, and temperament, as well as the handler's abilities. The best tools may also change throughout the training process. There is no one right piece of training equipment for every dog, and it's an individual choice. The best way to learn what works for your dog is to learn the proper way to use each tool, then give it a try. Let's take a look at some of the most common training tools.

CLICKERS

Clicker training is a type of marker training that often uses a small device called a clicker (or marker), which has a button that, when pressed, makes a clicking sound. Handlers use this sound to "mark" the exact moment the dog performs correctly, which is paired with a reward, such as a treat or a toy.

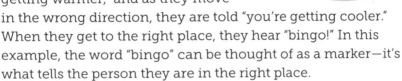

Think about the game "warmer, cooler" in which a person is moving about, and as they get closer to the correct spot, they are told "you're getting warmer," and as they move in the wrong direction, they are told "you're getting cooler." When they get to the right place, they hear "bingo!" In this example, the word "bingo" can be thought of as a marker—it's what tells the person they are in the right place.

Marker training works the same way. For example, if the goal is to teach the dog to touch a target of your hand, the moment the dog's nose makes contact with your hand it will be "marked" with a clicking sound and then rewarded. While the dog is reaching out toward the hand, you might say "good" as encouragement, but the marker does not come until their nose successfully touches the target—click!

You do not need to use a clicker for marker training. Many trainers and handlers prefer a verbal marker. A common verbal marker is the word "yes." It's short and clear. This can be easier than remembering to carry around a clicker, which may be too cumbersome for some to use.

The beauty of using a marker is that you have time to deliver the reward. It doesn't matter if it takes you several seconds longer to reach into your treat pouch or a few moments to throw a toy reward, because you have already "marked" the moment.

COLLARS

Collars are among the most common training tools around, allowing handlers to restrain dogs and offer corrections. Any puppy or adult dog can be outfitted with a simple buckle (flat) collar. However, other options offer a better fit and a bit more control than a standard buckle collar.

Martingale collars are a popular choice for any age of dog. A martingale is designed to constrict slightly with leash pressure and release again when the leash is loose, which allows you to give gentle, safe corrections. Its design prevents dogs from slipping free of the collar, which can happen more frequently with a standard flat-buckle collar.

Some handlers may choose to use a specialty training collar, such as a StarMark collar, which has plastic ridges, and is a step below a prong collar in terms of strength. Some trainers and handlers may choose to use a prong collar. When properly fitted and used correctly, they are an effective training tool that provides more precision and control with minimal strength needed on the part of the handler. Think of it as a leverage tool, sort of like power steering. As training progresses, you may phase out the prong collar in favor of a martingale or buckle collar, but the choice is ultimately up to the handler to decide what works best for themselves and their dog.

A choke chain is a classic slip collar that can fully constrict and release with a quick well-timed tug on the leash. Choke chains can work well for advanced-trained dogs that don't need a lot of collar direction or only need the occasional reminder. Otherwise, a choke chain may not be the best choice. For a similar chain action, try a chain martingale.

LEASHES

The standard dog leash is six feet long, which allows enough room for a dog to potty or walk freely. It can be held shorter when heeling with the dog near your side. The thickness of a leash depends on preference, with a thin (½-inch) leash often being easier to handle than a thick or heavy leash. There are also multipurpose leashes with extra clips designed to be worn cross-body; they don't require hands to hold the leash.

For working between on- and off-leash training, a short-tab is useful. This is a cord or leash segment that's like a handle, usually 6 to 12 inches long. A dog may wear a short-tab and collar when they're at home or off the leash. A longline is a 15-, 20-, or 30-foot leash used for exercise and training at a distance.

When choosing a leash, consider its material. A classic leather leash is most comfortable on the hands and breaks in nicely. Biothane leashes are a durable alternative to leather. Nylon leashes, while popular and inexpensive, can be harder on the hands and fray over time.

I recommend a six-foot leash for everyday use, a 15-foot longline, and a short-tab for wearing on the collar and when off-leash. A slip lead, which slips right over a dog's head and adjusts to any size, is also useful for training and walks.

HARNESSES

Some service dogs, such as mobility service dogs, wear specially made harnesses for bracing and balance support. These are usually custom-fitted to be comfortable and functional for physical tasking.

   Aside from mobility support or guide harnesses, body harnesses are not the best choice for general training or leash walking. This is because they don't give any control of a dog's head. If you have control of the head, you have control of the body. If the body is harnessed, the oppositional force is greater, such as when pulling a carriage. Therefore, harnesses work well for training a dog to pull, but if you want your dog to respond to leash pressure and follow the guidance of the leash, you may not want to choose a harness.

HEAD HALTERS

A head halter provides good control of a dog's direction. Head halters have been used to lead horses and other quadrupeds for thousands of years. When a dog goes to sniff or eat some-thing off the ground, a head halter requires minimal strength or force to prevent those behaviors. Be aware that it can take some time to get a dog acclimated to wearing a head halter.

Choose a brand that's designed to not put continual pressure on the dog's face when the leash has no tension. If a dog is very boisterous or tends to lunge and jump around on the leash, be careful when introducing a head halter to prevent risk of injury to the neck. A head halter should be used gently.

VESTS

Vests and capes are the most common working gear for service dogs. Although it's not legally required, most handlers choose to vest their dogs when working. The vest identifies to the public that the dog is not a pet—it's a service dog—and etiquette applies. A dog's gear can identify it more easily for public access. There are many types of vests and capes, including mesh capes  for warm weather and vests with packs on the side for carrying essentials. Some handlers choose to put patches on their dog's vest to identify what type of service dog it is, although this is not required. A simple vest or cape that says "Service Dog" may suffice, or you may choose more specific patches.

BAGS AND POUCHES

It's good to have treats within reach during the training process. A treat bag, also known as a bait bag, is a great way to keep your treats and toys close by. Bait bags designed to clip on to a belt are handy, especially the types that snap open and shut. A fanny pack can also work well as a training pouch.  Make sure the opening is large enough to quickly grab treats without too much fuss. Treats may be a dog's kibble or higher-value treats.

TWO
RULES AND TRAINING FOR YOUR SERVICE DOG

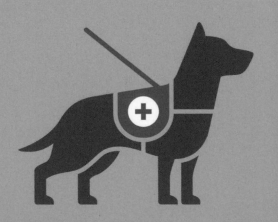

OBEDIENCE TRAINING doesn't just teach your dog practical skills and behaviors; it's the foundation of your dog's future education. Although it may be tempting to skip ahead to tasks and more advanced work, training must be built step-by-step. If we struggle at any step, we must ask ourselves if the dog truly understands what we're asking them to do. We don't expect small children to read before they learn the alphabet. Learning the basics prepares them for future learning. The same is true for service dogs.

22 HOUSE RULES

24 EXERCISE 1: SETTLE

26 EXERCISE 2: LEAVE IT

28 RULES FOR BEHAVING IN PUBLIC

30 EXERCISE 1: LOOK

32 EXERCISE 2: TOUCH

35 TEACHING A SERVICE DOG TO BE ON AND OFF THE CLOCK

38 EXERCISE 1: POTTY ON CUE

40 EXERCISE 2: PUTTING ON EQUIPMENT AND GEAR

Dogs need time and practice to generalize. A dog may understand "sit" and "down" in the living room but not outside. This is because the command has not been generalized yet. It's important to train within the home as well as in a variety of new environments. You will spend most of your time reviewing and practicing the exercises in this chapter, so your dog is prepared for more specialized training.

HOUSE RULES

House rules are the basic obedience skills your dog must master on their path toward public service. These are skills service dogs need to be useful, and they will use them every day. There are many basic house rules, but this section focuses on two of the most common ones: "settle" and "leave it."

Learning house rules is also an educational opportunity for handlers. Before getting started, take some time to familiarize yourself with how dogs learn. This includes how your dog reads body language and how they understand markers and praise.

Dogs are naturally readers of body language and are receptive to learning physical cues, such as hand signals—sometimes they learn these faster than they learn verbal cues. Feel free to pair hand signals or body cues with verbal commands, but always consider the final goal. For example, training your dog to "down" by pointing toward the floor may not work well in scenarios when your hands are full and you can't gesture. In that case, transitioning to a solid verbal command is most useful. You can do this by tapering off your cue, such as pointing farther from the ground each time you practice until it's faded into only a verbal cue. Plan to keep your cues consistent and track your dog's progress in your log on each exercise.

Clicker training (see page 15) with markers and rewards is an effective form of training, but praise is also an effective tool. A well-placed "good dog, nice job" when a dog is putting forth effort encourages them to keep going. Use praise and affection liberally when a dog is putting forth effort. Once they really get something right, throw a party. Let them genuinely know they've done something great. However, keep in mind that a marker is different than regular praise. Praise doesn't necessarily mean a dog will get a tangible reward, such as a treat. However, if they hear a click or a verbal "yes" marker, they should always receive a tangible reward.

Relatedly, you need to give feedback—a negative marker—when your dog gets things wrong. Do this gently as to not dampen the dog's desire to learn and try new things. There are different levels of negative markers. The first is "try again." This mild cue can be used consistently to let the dog know they don't have it right yet but should keep trying. It's more of an "oops" than a solid "no." A negative marker word, such as "no" or "ah-ah," is best used for behaviors that should completely stop. For example, if a dog goes to eat food off the ground outside, a firm and well-timed "no" can interrupt the behavior and let them know it's undesirable. Any time you correct your dog, try to redirect them to a behavior that is more desirable. Then you can follow up by praising them once they're switched over to doing something better.

HOUSE RULES EXERCISE 1:
SETTLE

What Does My Dog Need to Learn? Service dogs spend a good amount of time lying down quietly. Whether you are in class, seated at a restaurant, or waiting at the doctor's office, your dog should be able to quietly rest. As simple as it sounds, it's important that your dog can tune out distractions and not become restless.

Plan to ignore your dog for most of this exercise, although you may calmly check in via eye contact. To practice, pick a time in which you are quietly occupied, such as when reading a book or watching TV. Remember, you are shaping a calm, relaxed state. This is not a fun or exciting exercise for the dog, but they're learning how to "just be." Practice this "settle" exercise one to two times every day for at least 30 minutes at a time.

TRY THIS

1. With your dog on a leash, sit down somewhere you will be occupied and able to ignore your dog. Start in a relatively quiet place.

2. Use a mat to begin. A rubber-backed bathroom mat or a folded towel or blanket works well. This allows your dog to be comfortable and encourages them to lie down.

3. Place the mat down. Calmly praise your dog when they go onto the mat, while introducing them to the word "settle."

4. Have a seat, keeping your leash short enough so that the dog only has room to lie down. You may sit on the leash or hold it, whichever is easiest.

5. End the exercise only once your dog is calm and totally relaxed. Cue "free" or "all done," and calmly go about your activities.

6. Ready to practice in new places? Start with calm environments, which are easier, and as your dog does well, try more distracting places. Try "settle" at a friend's house or when other people are in the room at home. Once the dog has those down, practice in public places, such as a café, park bench, office, or any place you frequent.

? **Need Help?** If your dog becomes restless (whining, not lying down, soliciting attention) during practice, make sure all your dog's immediate needs have already been met and that they've been allowed to relieve themselves ahead of time. Begin practice in a low-distraction area. If all your dog's basic needs have been met and they're still restless, simply wait them out until they self-settle.

Is your dog trying to alert you to something? If you are also working on shaping any type of natural alerting, keep this in mind as you do this exercise. If you believe your dog is trying to alert you to something, such as an impending medical event, feel free to recognize and reward this. If all is okay, simply thank your dog for checking and remind them to "settle."

HOUSE RULES EXERCISE 2:
LEAVE IT

What Does My Dog Need to Learn? In real life, a service dog must ignore many smells and distractions. This starts with teaching impulse control with the "leave it" command. This command is also important when it comes to managing the environment. If a dog gets inadvertently rewarded for a behavior—such as finding a tasty morsel on the ground—the behavior is reinforced. You want to avoid this scenario whenever possible. Teaching a solid "leave it" can start in the home. Difficulty level can increase, leading to setting up a "leave it" obstacle course outside.

TRY THIS

1. Choose an item for your "leave it." This should be something desirable to your dog, but not something they can quickly consume if they accidentally get it. A large dog biscuit or hardened stale bread works well to start.

2. Have your training treats on hand, ready to reward your dog.

3. Starting with your dog on-leash, say "leave it" as you slowly place the forbidden item on the ground. Use the leash to prevent the dog from contacting the item.

4. When your dog ignores the item or gives up interest in attempting to sniff it, mark (using your clicker or saying yes) and reward from your treat pouch. Be careful that your dog doesn't go back to take the item you set on the ground.

5. Practice until you can place the item on the ground with the leash dropped.

6. Vary the items you use: hot dogs, paper towels, toys—anything that might be interesting to your dog. Next, try a surprise "leave it" while your dog is settled on their mat or on a down stay to simulate food falling off a table in a restaurant.

7. Simulate a "leave it" obstacle course inside or outside. Place items in advance, or have a helper lay some things out for you. Then put your obedience skills and "leave it" to the test as you handle your dog, rewarding them for desired behaviors and obedience.

? **Need Help?** A dog that is highly excited by food items may need to spend more time on steps 1 through 4. If your dog is too excited by the food at first, try using a less valuable item. For example, a banana peel is interesting, but less exciting than a piece of meat or cheese. This gives you the opportunity to reward your dog once they ignore the item. If you can't place the "leave it" items on the ground, place them on a higher surface, such as a chair or coffee table. If your dog is too persistent, try to use your hand, palm down and fingers extended like claws, to form a "cage" over the item. When working on-leash near items on the ground, remember to say "leave it" right as your dog approaches the item.

RULES FOR BEHAVING IN PUBLIC

The term "public access" means service dogs accompany their handlers in all public places. They need extra socialization and training for all the things they will encounter in public. Experts say that at least 30 hours of a service dog's total training time should focus on dealing with unexpected surprises and other distractions in public.

Think about a typical puppy. They bounce out of the house, dragging their handler behind them as they frolic down the sidewalk sniffing each bush. They discover a discarded chicken bone on the ground and gobble it down. Across the street, they see a squirrel and take off running after it. The squirrel escapes, but it was a fun chase. At the local pet-friendly store, the pup gets celebrity treatment. Everyone wants to shower them with affection and treats. As they jump all over them, they praise the dog. They excitedly sniff each new person for treats. On the way home, the puppy passes several other dogs on walks. They pull and lunge toward the dogs, so the handler allows them to stop and say hi. Most of the dogs they meet are friendly, but one dog doesn't like puppies. As they bounce up to the new dog, they are received with a growl and a snap to their face.

Note each time the puppy receives something rewarding or something negative, both of which reinforce behavior. Service dogs must be constantly engaged with and focused on their handler, not all the goings-on of the world, as a typical puppy might be. As you socialize and train your dog for public access, the priority is to expose them to new things in a positive manner, while maintaining good manners and keeping them safe. Use your judgment to ensure any human and dog interactions are positive ones. In this section, we focus on two important engagement exercises: "look" and "touch."

ENGAGEMENT EXERCISE 1:
LOOK

What Does My Dog Need to Learn? This is a simple but meaningful foundational obedience exercise, suitable for both a puppy and an adult. Your dog will visually focus on your face and be rewarded for making (and maintaining) eye contact with you, while ignoring distractions.

When practiced regularly, this skill gives you the ability to regain your dog's attention and focus in different situations. A reliable "look" cue can be very useful when distractions occur in public places.

Start this exercise at home, either sitting down or standing. If you are practicing outdoors, use a leash and collar to keep your pup on task, should they try to wander. Your dog can be in any position, but it's best to practice with your pup in the position in which they would most often be in public, such as at your designated "heel" side. Limit this exercise to three times a day for about five minutes or less each time to avoid burnout or boredom.

TRY THIS

1. Holding a small treat inside one hand, allow your dog to briefly smell the food and become interested.

2. Draw your lure hand up toward the side of your face, near your temple, as you say the cue "look." Verbally praise your dog as they look up and make eye contact with you.

3. Starting with just a few seconds of eye contact, mark (using your clicker or saying yes) and reward by giving your dog the treat you had in your hand. Repeat this process.

4. Begin to add the verbal cue "look" as you lure the treat toward your face. You may also use your dog's name to get their attention before the cue.

5. As you progress, practice in new places and around new distractions. Slowly increase the length of time your dog must look at you before they receive the treat. (Remember the three Ds: distance, duration, and distraction.)

6. As you practice, phase out the lure. Once your dog no longer needs the visual hand signal and understands they are rewarded for eye contact, simply use the verbal cue.

? **Need Help?** If your dog isn't interested in the treat, try small pieces of a higher-value treat or train your dog using parts of their daily meals. The best time to train is when a dog is hungry before their usual mealtime. You can also try nonfood rewards, such as a favorite toy or anything your dog enjoys.

If your dog only looks at the treat and doesn't offer eye contact, remember to only mark at the moment your dog makes eye contact with you. This marker tells the dog they are doing the right thing at the exact moment. A little trick to getting eye contact in the beginning is to blow a puff of air toward your dog, so they look up.

ENGAGEMENT EXERCISE 2: TOUCH

What Does My Dog Need to Learn? A nose touch is a good bonding exercise, as well as a skill for future service tasks and alerts, such as closing a door, pushing a button, and alerting a handler to an event. Since dogs don't have hands, they can use their noses, mouths, or paws to perform a task. Many dogs will offer paws quite readily, but the disadvantage to pawing is that it can scratch objects or the handler's skin. Barking is typically an undesirable alert for a service dog, because it is disruptive. Most often, dogs are taught to use their nose to touch instead. Later on, you can teach the dog to touch various targets. Most dogs find this exercise easy in the beginning, and quite engaging. Imagine a dog learning to push a button and receive a treat. The "button" is whatever the target is, in this case your hand. Practice this exercise several times a day for about five minutes each time.

TRY THIS

1. Keep a leash on your dog as you practice to keep them on task. You may do the exercise seated, standing, or from any position where your dog can reach your hand.

2. Choose one hand to begin. Briefly hold a treat in that hand, then remove the treat and set it aside. (This is just to get a bit of the scent of food on your hand to draw the dog's interest.)

3. Present your hand, with a fist or open palm, one to two feet in front of your dog's face. Be ready to quickly mark (using your clicker or saying yes) the moment their nose touches your hand.

4. Pause for a few moments and repeat. Mark and reward each time your dog's nose touches your hand. Praise your dog.

5. Your hand signal for "touch" will be a quick and distinctive hand movement. You can rotate your wrist back and forth in a motion as if saying "so-so." Or if it's easier, you can wiggle your fingers. This signal will also serve as a silent cue for "touch."

6. Repeat this exercise about 10 times, keeping it fun and simple by presenting your hand the same way every time.

7. Once your dog has mastered touching your hand in front of them, make it more difficult. Present your hand higher or lower. Switch and present your other hand. Practice so that no matter where your hand is, your dog will touch it. Generalize the behavior by practicing in new environments and with distractions around.

8. It is helpful to train a dog to be eager to repeat a behavior on cue and not always expect a reward after one single attempt at the behavior. As your dog becomes confident in "touch," begin to vary your reward frequency. For example, sometimes you'll reward after one good solid "touch," and sometimes you'll simply praise "good job," repeat "touch," and have them keep going to two or three repetitions before marking and rewarding.

9. If your goal is to have a pushier type of touch alert, or if you'll desire a stronger nudge to train as an alert in the future, try this: Hold a treat in your closed fist. When the dog pushes your fist trying to get the treat, praise them. Once they've pushed and tried for several seconds, mark and reward by opening your hand. As you continue to practice, shape the behavior by only rewarding for the "touch" repetitions that push your hand.

? **Need Help?** It's common for dogs to attempt to "give paw" or offer another behavior when asked to "touch." If your dog gives the wrong behavior, do not reward for it. Ignore the incorrect attempt and simply say "try again" until you get a nose touch. If your dog is overly interested in the treats and ignores your hand, try placing the treats a bit farther away from where your hand is. If your dog becomes confused as you move your hand or switch hands, go back a step to the last thing they were successful at.

TEACHING A SERVICE DOG TO BE ON AND OFF THE CLOCK

All service dogs (or dogs in training) have "on the clock" time when they are at work and "off the clock" time when they are engaged in a nonwork activity that occupies their attention. For example, you might meet up with a friend and her dog, allowing both dogs to play off-leash and romp around. It's important to teach your dog to distinguish between work time and free time, and there are some cues you can use to accomplish this.

To indicate to a dog that they are on the clock, training equipment—vests, collar, leash, etc.—can cue a dog that it's time to work and that their focus should be on you. Cues indicating free time may include removing the vest or using a cue like "free," followed by encouraging the dog to play or explore. The goal is to make things clear.

When the vest is on, it's business time, with a higher expectation for behavior. Any distracting activities, sniffing, or interaction with others should be prevented. The exact amount of time a service dog is off the clock depends on the individual situation. A puppy will need more time off. One thing is for certain, all dogs need time to just be dogs. A healthy balance of work, play, and plenty of rest is vital to your dog's well-being.

Although you should consistently train with equipment, your dog's good behavior shouldn't, for example, depend on a vest, as there will be times they'll need to work without a vest or leash. Occasionally practice obedience and tasks when your dog is not wearing a vest.

Another key part of teaching your service dog when they are on and off the clock is being consistent about who is giving commands. A typical family pet may have similar bonds with—and get attention from—multiple people. However, a service dog needs to know who they are working for (the handler) and have a strong bond with that person. Negotiating this depends on your family structure and your abilities to train, walk, and provide care.

It's best to have one main handler for training and to make sure everyone in the household is on the same page. When the dog is "off the clock," someone else can fill in as a caretaker, but they should avoid giving commands—especially commands the dog is still learning—and stick to only reinforcing good manners, such as not pulling on the lead and politely going through doorways.

ON/OFF CLOCK EXERCISE 1:
POTTY ON CUE

What Does My Dog Need to Learn? It's important to train your dog to only relieve themselves on cue and never when they're on the clock. Giving appropriately timed breaks outside will help prevent any accidents in public places. Your dog will learn to go on command when they are on a leash (held slack) and to overcome preferences about where they currently potty. You'll need treats, a six-foot leash, and waste baggies. If you normally vest your dog for outings, skip the vest when you're first training this exercise. Ultimately it won't matter if the vest is on or off; the command will let them know when it's time.

TRY THIS

1. Pick verbal cues, such as "go potty" (urinating) and "business" (defecating), to indicate when your dog should relieve themselves. Pick a training time when they are likely to have to relieve themselves. First thing in the morning always works.

2. With your dog leashed and under control ("heel" command), walk outside to an area you'd normally take your dog to potty. Don't let them potty yet! Keep their nose off the ground and their head up with focus on you, controlling the walk so they stay on task for at least two minutes or more (less if they have to go urgently).

3. Approach the spot you want them to go, pause for a moment, and ask for a behavior such as "look" or a sit-stay. Free your dog by slacking the leash out, allowing your dog to have the full length to sniff around, and say your verbal cue.

4. If you normally hold the leash in your left hand with your dog on your left side, switch the leash to your opposite hand. Make it boring. Don't allow the dog to take you for a long walk. Keep slowly pacing back and forth over the same area, as you repeat your verbal cue every so often.

5. As soon as your dog begins to potty, mark and reward with a treat and lots of happy praise and a walk as soon as they finish.

6. Practice on as many different surfaces as your dog might encounter later on, such as concrete or a small patch of dirt.

Need Help? If your dog is unclear on when they are "free" to go sniff around and potty, gesture them toward the potty area and immediately praise when they begin to sniff. Some dogs take a long time to potty. A clever dog might have learned that the longer they hold out, the farther their owner will walk them. You want your dog to get the idea that potty business happens first, followed by the walk as the reward.

ON/OFF CLOCK EXERCISE 2:
PUTTING ON EQUIPMENT AND GEAR

What Does My Dog Need to Learn? Putting a collar, harness, or vest on an excited wiggly dog can be like trying to put a sweater on an octopus. Your dog will learn to put their head through their own collar and stand still for equipment such as a cape, vest, or backpack.

TRY THIS

1. Don't hype up walk time. Dogs feed on our emotions. Counter that energy by being calm and patient and using a soft voice.

2. Start with the collar. In one hand, hold the collar in a loop in front of your dog's head. On the opposite side of the collar, hold up a treat with your other hand.

3. Lure your dog to move forward a step and slip their head through the collar to get the treat. (If you train with a prong collar, skip this step, as it can injure a dog's eyes.)

4. Once your dog gets the idea, fade or decrease the use of the food lure, praising your dog when they put their head through the collar.

5. Next train your dog to stand-stay for a vest, cape, backpack, or similar. Hold a treat in front of and slightly above your dog's head and say your "stand-stay" command. If your dog sits, lure them forward until they're standing, then mark and reward.

6. Set the vest on their back, and if they maintain the stay, mark and reward. If they break the stay position, lure them back into the desired position before the next step.

7. Secure the straps or buckles, then follow with praise.

Need Help? Make sure your dog's vest or pack fits well and isn't causing discomfort. In general, two fingers should fit between the vest and the dog's body. If it's uncomfortable, they won't want to wear it. If your dog is still overly excited or isn't cooperating after a couple tries, halt the process, walk away, and set down your gear. Dogs do not like fun things to be delayed. Your dog will learn that calm behavior is not optional, it's a requirement, and the fastest way to move on to all the good things (like training and walks) is to cooperate calmly. Try again once your dog has calmed down.

THREE
GENERAL SERVICE DOG TASKS

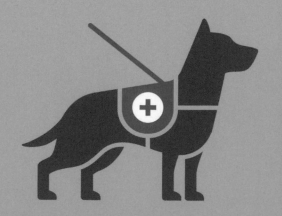

SERVICE DOGS can be trained to perform tasks based on the handler's needs. Therefore, many dogs are cross-trained for multiple purposes, and some tasks, like the ones in this chapter, serve multiple purposes or are building blocks for more complex tasks. You'll see tasks are grouped into basic categories by their primary function, such as retrieve or open/close, and then broken down further into specific tasks. You will notice some skills overlap, and some might give you ideas for new tasks. Each task includes labels that specify the type of service dog (see page 5) associated with the skill, making it easy to focus training.

44 CARRYING AND RETRIEVING TASKS

46 TASK 1: INTRODUCING FETCH GAMES

48 TASK 2: SHAPING THE RETRIEVE USING A DUMBBELL

50 TASK 3: "TAKE IT" AND "HOLD IT"

52 TASK 4: "BRING": THE FORMAL RETRIEVE

54 TASK 5: INTRODUCING NEW RETRIEVE/CARRY ITEMS

56 OPENING AND CLOSING TASKS

58 TASK 1: PULLING TO DRAG OBJECTS

60 TASK 2: TOUCHING A TARGET

62 TASK 3: PAW-PUSH TARGETING

64 TASK 4: OPENING AND CLOSING A DOOR

66 TASK 5: TURNING LIGHTS ON AND OFF

68 OTHER GENERAL TASKS

70 TASK 1: ASSISTING WITH LAUNDRY

72 TASK 2: ASSISTING WITH CLOTHING REMOVAL

74 TASK 3: BRINGING A DRINK FROM THE FRIDGE

76 TASK 4: BRINGING A DOG BOWL AND PLACING IT ON THE COUNTERTOP

79 TASK 5: TAKING A RECEIPT FROM A CASHIER AND DELIVERING IT TO A HANDLER

CARRYING AND RETRIEVING TASKS

Retrieving is a key behavior for service dogs and the basis for many other tasks. The end goal of the formal retrieve has three parts: (1) the dog reliably picks up various objects, (2) the dog holds and carries objects in their mouth, and (3) the dog delivers the objects to your hand. The result is a trained behavior done on command as obedience, not as play, which is why it's called a "formal retrieve" and not "fetch."

Like many tasks, retrieve is "shaped," which means it's put together piece by piece and that the beginning doesn't always look like the end. Each lesson in this section starts with its own criteria or goal, and each builds on the one that came before. We shape a task using marker training (see page 15) and raising criteria. Look for an 80 percent successful response rate before moving to the next step.

As we shape behaviors, we also try to minimize letting the dog practice the skill incorrectly. It's easier to prevent a bad habit than correct one later. For example, you wouldn't want a dog to pick up a retrieve item, then go lie down and chew on it. This can be prevented by immediately calling the dog when they have the item and not allowing any time for them to take it elsewhere, drop it, or chew on it. When in doubt, keep a collar and leash on your dog so you can gain control when needed.

Each dog has its own level of aptitude for learning new things, and there are many ways to train the retrieve. If one way isn't working, you may need to try a different approach or spend more time on a particular step.

TASK 1:
INTRODUCING FETCH GAMES

What Does My Dog Need to Learn? Fetch games are beneficial to any dog, regardless of age, size, or breed. They build your dog's desire to interact with you and bring you things. Games with toys tap into prey drive (the dog's innate instinct to chase moving things). This is not a formal retrieve, but rather a fun game to build motivation. Revisit this exercise throughout the training process as part of your lasting routine of ending each obedience and task training session with a game and play. It's also a great way to give your dog some sprinting exercise.

TRY THIS

1. Choose two similar toys that your dog likes, such as tug toys, ball on a rope, or segments of rubber hose—no food rewards are needed.

2. If possible, start in a long hallway where the dog will have no other options but to come back to you. Avoid playing fetch on slippery flooring.

3. Show your dog the toy and get them excited for it. Build interest by briefly tossing it around, keeping it just out of their reach.

4. Enthusiastically toss the toy and encourage your dog to go get it.

5. When your dog picks up the toy, show them the second toy (in your hand) as you call them back using an informal cue, such as "pup, pup, pup!" If possible, walk backward or move away from your dog as they bring the toy while encouraging them to return to you.

6. When they return to you, praise them and toss the second toy.

7. Pick up the toy your dog has dropped, or have a second person grab it for you. If you won't be able to get the second toy off the ground, consider attaching a long thin line (such as clothesline or a 15- to 20-foot leash) to the toy so you can reel it back in after it's thrown.

8. Optionally, add a short game of tug when your dog brings the toy back.

9. End the game by cuing your dog "all done" to end any play or training session. Put the toys away, preferably in your jacket or pocket.

? **Need Help?** If your dog doesn't show interest in the toys, try different types and textures. Increase drive for the toy by attaching a line or leash to the toy and dragging it around on the ground, similar to a cat toy. The idea is similar for any predatory animal: get the object moving around quickly just out of reach in jerky movements, engaging the desire to chase and catch it. Also try limiting your dog's access to toys in the house. Scarcity increases desire. Limit toys to the daily times you play interactively.

TASK 2:
SHAPING THE RETRIEVE USING A DUMBBELL

What Does My Dog Need to Learn? The retrieve is trained using marker training and shaping each successive attempt. Many repetitions and rewards are done before raising the criteria or moving on to the next step. You need a single retrieve item to consistently practice with. You will use this to train for an extended length of time before introducing other items. A plastic training dumbbell is preferred, as it's easy for a dog to pick up off a flat surface. If a dumbbell is not accessible to you, use an object that is medium weight, comfortable for your dog to pick up and hold, and longer than the width of your dog's mouth, such as a wooden or plastic dowel or a segment of rubber hose. Start slow by making a positive association with the dumbbell and encouraging your dog to interact with it. Remember, the dumbbell is not a toy and should be put away when you're not in a training session. However, once you take it out, a fun attitude will help get your dog excited to train.

TRY THIS

1. From a sitting position with your dog in front of you, present the dumbbell in front of your dog, about a foot away from their face, and encourage your dog to check it out.

2. Mark and reward each time your dog touches the dumbbell in any way. If they sniff it or nudge it, mark and reward them with food.

3. Repeat this five to six times, presenting the dumbbell as you put a verbal cue to the object, such as "wanna dumbbell" in a happy tone of voice.

4. If your dog paws at the dumbbell, simply ignore and say "try again." Only reward for contact they make with their nose or mouth.

5. Always end sessions on a high note, before the dog becomes bored with the exercise.

6. Take your time repeating this exercise once daily, until your dog readily touches the dumbbell to be rewarded.

7. Next, reward the dog for putting their mouth on the dumbbell in any way, even for a split second. Try moving it around as you hold it, encouraging your dog to take it. When they put their mouth on it, immediately mark and reward and use heavy praise. Do this for at least a week or more, depending on how fast your dog learns.

? **Need Help?** If your dog is not making contact with the dumbbell, try directing them by tapping the middle area of the dumbbell with your finger. They should figure out fairly quickly that touching it results in a "yes" or click, and a reward. If your dog begins to bark out of frustration, or if you get frustrated, set the dumbbell down next to you and take a break. Present it again, ready to mark and reward when they touch it. If after two weeks of sessions your dog hasn't put their mouth on it yet, try gently placing it in their mouth and quickly mark and reward. Do this until they offer the behavior on their own.

TASK 3:
"TAKE IT" AND "HOLD IT"

What Does My Dog Need to Learn? At this point, your dog has been consistently rewarded for touching the dumbbell and heavily rewarded for putting their mouth on it. Your dog sees the exercise as fun and interesting, and now we will add some additional steps to work toward a formal retrieve. There are two goals to keep in mind: (1) the dog shows initiative to take the item with their mouth while you're holding it, and (2) the dog learns to hold it in their mouth for increasing lengths of time. Expect to practice these steps over a period of several weeks, with additional time to generalize in new places, positions, and around distractions.

TRY THIS

1. While seated with your dog in front of you, present the dumbbell about a foot in front of your dog at their eye level.

2. When they put their mouth on the middle of the dumbbell or grip it, mark and reward.

3. If your dog is not grabbing the dumbbell with their mouth, try gently placing it into their mouth, and quickly mark and reward. Then try again.

4. Once your dog gets it and has at least three successful attempts in a row (that you've rewarded), introduce the verbal cue "take it."

5. Present the dumbbell as you say "take it." Mark and reward when the dog takes it.

6. Once your dog successfully puts their mouth on the dumbbell at least eight out of 10 times it's presented, introduce the verbal cue "hold it."

7. To start "hold it," after your dog takes the dumbbell in their mouth, place your other hand under your dog's chin to steady them. Start with just a second or two, and mark and reward. Continue to use your hand to steady their chin as needed, until you see they are gripping the dumbbell on their own.

8. Build up the duration by encouraging your dog to "hold it," adding just a few seconds at a time in each session.

9. If your dog drops the dumbbell, pick it up and try again. Try to only mark while the dog is still holding it.

10. Make sure to practice "take it" from different positions. Once your dog successfully takes the dumbbell from your hand when it's presented, try offering it from slightly farther away, lower toward the ground, and slightly above their head.

11. Feel free to mix it up and use other "life rewards" besides food. Put the dumbbell in your pocket, and when your dog is standing by the door excited to go outside, take the dumbbell out and ask for a five-second hold. Mark and immediately open the door to let them outside. The dumbbell hold is your dog's key to all things good.

? Need Help? If any steps are difficult, go back to the previous step and move in slower increments. If your dog is dropping the dumbbell too quickly, don't mark and reward. Ask for a second "hold" and only reward when the dog hangs on for a moment longer. Get them used to your hand cradling their chin by having your dog sit in front of you as you encourage them to rest their head with three or four fingers under their chin.

TASK 4:
"BRING": THE FORMAL RETRIEVE

What Does My Dog Need to Learn? Once your dog reliably takes and holds items out of your hand, the next step is adding motion to it. You will work toward getting your dog to pick up and carry the object to you from different places, both high and low. This will be the first time your dog retrieves the dumbbell from someplace other than your hands.

TRY THIS

1. Begin by going over the last step your dog was successful at. Mark and reward your dog for taking the dumbbell from your hand and holding it, with the bar just behind their canines.

2. Next, practice "take it" from someplace other than your hand by setting the dumbbell on a surface, such as a chair or low table, placed in front of your dog. Try to keep the dumbbell at the same level at which you presented it.

3. Encourage your dog to "take it," then mark and reward when successful.

4. Repeat this process, ending the session after a successful attempt to finish on a high note.

5. Once your dog can pick up the item from the surface three times in a row, you are ready to add motion to the hold by introducing the formal command "bring it."

6. Set the dumbbell on a surface as in step 2. Stand or sit two or three paces from your dog and cue them to "take it."

7. Introduce the command "bring it" as you encourage them to come to you and deliver it to your hand.

8. Introduce the "out" command as the dog lets go. You may choose to label this as "give" or "drop."

9. When the dog delivers to your hand, give super enthusiastic praise.

? **Need Help?** If your dog drops the retrieve item while beginning to learn to carry it, try to encourage your dog to pick it back up on their own, then continue. Point at the dumbbell and say "take it," then try again. Keep your sessions brief, especially if your dog finds this work mentally taxing in the beginning. Remember, your dog is figuring out pieces to the puzzle, and it can take a lot of repetitions before it all clicks one day.

TASK 5:
INTRODUCING NEW RETRIEVE/CARRY ITEMS

What Does My Dog Need to Learn? Once you have taught your dog how to retrieve the dumbbell, you can introduce new, more challenging items. Every dog is different, and some can be picky about what objects they take at first. Many objects can be adapted for your dog or modified in simple ways to be more comfortable for the dog to carry. For example, a rough wicker basket with a handle can be modified by wrapping electrical tape around the area the dog grips. Some dogs are reluctant to retrieve metal items at first. Keys can be modified by adding a leather keychain tab for the dog to grip. Your cell phone can be easily damaged by a dog's teeth, saliva, or accidentally dropped, so it's best to get a sturdy protective case for your phone before introducing it. Create a list of items your dog has been introduced to, and keep progress notes in your training log.

TRY THIS

1. Choose a few items that you'd like your dog to learn to retrieve or carry. Some common items are a medication bag, phone, keys, and a drink.

2. One at a time, set these items out on a low table, a chair, or the floor, and let your dog check them out. Stick to introducing only one new item per training session.

3. Always begin a step back in the process. With each new item, you will not cue "bring it" right away. Go back to the step prior, in which you were still holding the item in your hand, asking your dog to "take it."

4. Present the new item in your hand as you cue "take it," and mark and reward for the dog putting their mouth on it. In the next set of reps, reward for holding it progressively longer.

5. As an option, verbally name each new item as you pick it up and present it. Your dog can learn to discern many objects by name and smell.

6. Take extra time to practice holds with more delicate items, such as a slip of paper, a letter (junk mail), or a credit card (use an old credit card for practice).

7. When you first introduce a can of soda or water bottle, start with room temperature, as some dogs don't like cold at first. Avoid teaching your dog to retrieve bottles made from glass, items that are easily punctured, or items with sharp edges. If introducing medication bottles, make sure they have child-proof lids securely attached or keep them inside a pouch.

Need Help? If your dog is chomping or chewing an item, that is undesirable. Only mark and reward for a quiet hold. Keep your hand on the object until it's steady, then briefly take your hand off as your dog holds it in front of you. If your dog is grabbing the item, then spitting it out too quickly without holding it, keep the item still in your hand and do nothing. Then cue your dog again, rewarding only a longer hold.

OPENING AND CLOSING TASKS

Opening and closing tasks can be taught to help service dogs assist a handler living with mobility issues. Common tasks include opening and closing doors, cabinets, refrigerators, and more. Like formal retrieves, opening and closing skills can be chained together to achieve many different specific tasks. Get ready to think creatively to come up with tasks that can best help you. Objects that will be opened and closed can be adapted to your dog's abilities by attaching a pull handle. If your dog will naturally tug or pull on a toy, you will have an easier time teaching this. Their size and physical build factor into what they are able to pull, so modify according to your dog's abilities.

TASK 1:
PULLING TO DRAG OBJECTS

What Does My Dog Need to Learn? Teaching your dog to pull a handle on command is the foundation of several tasks, including opening doors, refrigerators, and cabinets. Pulling is used to drag an object like a duffel bag or things that are generally too heavy for the dog to pick up. Tugging is a skill needed for more complex tasks, such as assisting a handler in removing clothing. You'll need a handle your dog can grab with their mouth and tug on. Special service dog handles are available online, but feel free to use something you already have at home, such as a short segment of rope, a hand towel, or a large nylon dog collar that is easy to knot.

TRY THIS

1. Introduce the exercise by holding the handle in your hand as you playfully encourage your dog to grab on to it.

2. If your dog needs more encouragement to grip the handle, use your "take it" cue from the retrieval tasks section (see page 50).

3. As your dog tugs or pulls the handle, praise them and slowly release the handle from your hand, then mark and reward.

4. Repeat step 3 over several days or more, until your dog will readily pull the handle out of your hand when you present it.

5. Next, attach the handle to an object on which your dog can practice dragging, such as a laundry basket, suitcase, grocery bag, or duffel bag. If using a laundry basket, add something to it to give it the desired weight to pull.

6. With the handle on the laundry basket, pick up the handle and encourage your dog to "take it" and "pull" as you stand or sit behind them.

7. Once your dog shows any effort to drag the basket, mark and reward and praise.

8. Practice from farther away. Place your dog in a stay command several feet from the basket. Show them the handle by picking it up in your hand.

9. Return to your dog, and cue "go pull" in an enthusiastic manner.

10. Once your dog can pull the basket a few feet, work on introducing new items.

> **?** **Need Help?** If your dog will grab but won't pull, go back to the earlier step of using the pull handle like a toy, encouraging your dog to pull it out of your hands on cue. Get them excited to play the game.

TASK 2:
TOUCHING A TARGET

What Does My Dog Need to Learn? We have covered how to teach "touch" as a nose push to the target of your hand (see page 32), which is a foundational skill for many different "closing the door" exercises. Now you will "move" the target onto another object. By teaching the dog to "touch" a piece of tape or sticky note on our hand, we can then transfer that target to different objects as a guide for the dog. Wide blue painter's tape is preferable, as dogs see the color blue most easily when contrasted against other surfaces. Plus, this type of tape won't damage surfaces, and a roll should last a good amount of time.

TRY THIS

1. As a refresher, practice the "touch" engagement exercise (see page 32), marking and rewarding when your dog makes contact with your hand or fist, from various positions.

2. To shape the best touch or alert, encourage and reward firm pushes from the dog. Vary how many pushes the dog must do before getting the reward, from one to two or three in a row.

3. Take a piece of blue tape, about the size of your palm, and stick it to your hand.

4. Present your outstretched hand, palm up, with the tape as a target, and cue your dog to "touch." Mark and reward when your dog nose-touches the tape on your hand.

5. When your dog successfully noses the tape eight out of 10 attempts, it's time to transfer the target. To begin, choose a surface that's at your dog's eye level, such as the kitchen drawer.

6. To bridge between touching the tape on the hand and touching the tape on the drawer, place your hand, palm-side up with the tape on it, flat against the front of the drawer. Cue your dog to "touch," and mark and reward. Repeat this several times.

7. When your dog is consistently successful, transfer the tape to the cabinet, right where your hand was.

8. Briefly tap the tape, as you say "touch target." Mark and reward for any touch to the tape.

9. Shape the behavior by encouraging your dog to push firmly enough to close the open drawer. Do this by opening the drawer, cuing "touch target," and only rewarding successively firm pushes.

10. Once your dog can touch and push the tape target on a drawer, move the target to a new place or add a second target. Repeat steps 1 through 9 each time you introduce a new object.

? **Need Help?** If your dog does not understand to touch the target after you transfer it to the drawer or other surface, go back a step and keep practicing with the tape on your hand in front of the object.

TASK 3:
PAW-PUSH TARGETING

What Does My Dog Need to Learn? Aside from a nose-touch (see page 32), dogs can also use their paws for various tasks and handler alerts. Here, your dog will learn to touch their paw to, or "paw-push," a target. This task is not for everyone: a paw has nails, and depending on the dog and handler, it may be undesirable for a dog to use their paws, as it can scratch the handler's body or damage delicate surfaces. If you already taught "touch" as a nose-touch, keep nose-touch and paw-push as different commands. You may say "paws" instead of "touch," or use any command that works for you, as long as you keep it consistent.

TRY THIS

1. From a sitting position or on the ground, with your dog in front of you or at your side, hold a piece of food inside your hand as you make a fist.

2. Place your hand low in front of your dog, just a bit above the floor.

3. Encourage your dog to "get it" as you move your hand around a bit to build some interest and mild frustration. As soon as your dog paws at your hand, mark and reward by opening your hand to give them the treat.

4. Once your dog consistently performs step 3, transfer the "paw" behavior to an object. Present the object in front of your dog, tapping it as you say "paw." Mark and reward when they paw at the desired target.

Need Help? If your dog is not offering the paw, try a different approach. Place your hand, palm up, on the floor in front of your dog, and move it around until you can capture the behavior with a marker. If your dog is having trouble pawing a target, try moving the target lower until you get more successful repetitions.

TASK 4:
OPENING AND CLOSING A DOOR

What Does My Dog Need to Learn? This task combines the "pull" and "touch a target" tasks. These commands are chained together to teach a dog to assist a handler by opening and closing a door, sliding door, cabinet door, or kitchen drawers. This behavior can also be applied to laundry (washer or dryer doors) with a special modified handle.

TRY THIS

1. Choose a door that is not too heavy. Check it out yourself, opening and closing the door to make sure there is enough room for your dog to practice. Take extra care that the door does not swing too far or hit the wall when pulled open. Anything that startles or scares your dog can really set back the training process. If necessary, use your hands, your foot, or prop up pillows to control how fast the door can swing.

2. Attach a pull handle to a door handle. Allow your dog to see you doing this. If your dog is smaller or shorter, use a longer handle or a leash.

3. Show them the handle and cue them to "take it" and "pull." Mark and reward each time the dog moves the door.

4. During the training process, between sessions, remove the handle from the door or cabinets when you're not using it. Once your dog understands and can perform the task reliably, handles can be left on anything the dog will need to open.

Need Help? Some dogs will pull a door handle just a bit too enthusiastically and will continue to pull the handle like a toy, even once the door is open. Mark and reward your dog before they have a chance to continue to pull on the handle. Teaching a solid "out" command, or "drop it," is very useful in this situation.

TASK 5:
TURNING LIGHTS ON AND OFF

What Does My Dog Need to Learn? Teaching light switches often requires some special adaptations for the dog. The easiest way is by using a prop light switch affixed to a movable piece of wooden board. This way the switch on a board can be held in front of the dog, or propped lower against the wall as the dog learns the mechanics of flipping it up or down, before attempting it on a higher wall switch. If your home has a special type of light switch, buy that type and affix to a board about the height of your dog's head. If you start by training on an actual wall switch, keep in mind your wall may get some scratches. If that is an issue, you might want to put up something protective before beginning.

TRY THIS

1. If necessary, add a small extension to the switch so the dog can more easily manipulate it. This can be gradually made smaller, until the dog can flip the regular switch. Rubber tubing that fits snugly over the switch or a rolled segment of duct tape works well to extend the switch anywhere from ¼ to two inches.

2. Cue your dog to "touch target" the switch as you tap it with your finger. This cue is just to let your dog know how to start doing it.

3. As you introduce the switch in the first lesson, mark and reward each time your dog touches the switch.

4. Once you have their attention, show them how the switch flips both up and down, by flipping it yourself. Lights turn on or off by touching the switch either from underneath or from above.

5. Encourage your dog to touch the switch from underneath, or above, by lightly tapping that area as you give your cue. The extension you've placed on the switch will help greatly with making it clear to your dog.

6. From your second session forward, reward only when the dog flips the switch to the opposite position. If your dog touches it but doesn't flip it, use encouragement to get your dog to keep trying again. Praise them for each try, but only reward with food if the switch is flipped.

7. Once they're getting the idea, choose a cue to put to the exercise, such as "lights." If you have taught this using a switch on a board, you may now prop the board against the wall and practice. At this time, you can also try changing to a smaller extension or none at all, depending on what works best for your dog. You may transition to a higher wall switch as soon as your dog is confident and having success with the prop light switch.

? **Need Help?** In order to reach a typical wall switch, if a dog is too short when standing on their rear legs, they will need a platform or steady chair to step up on, placed under the switch. Practice that separately. There are also special light switch extenders that may be useful for a smaller dog.

OTHER GENERAL TASKS

More complex tasks are often chains of behaviors put together in different ways. This requires a dog to have some mastery of each step and the encouragement to keep going and piece it all together. Now that your dog has a foundational set of skills, you can combine them to perform a sequence for various types of tasks, such as gathering and moving items like laundry or trash, retrieving more difficult items like drinks and shopping receipts, and more.

TASK 1:
ASSISTING WITH LAUNDRY

What Does My Dog Need to Learn? Your dog will learn to pick up or retrieve items of clothing, transfer them to another place you indicate, and release them. Prerequisite skills include "take it" (see page 50), "bring it" (see page 52), and "out" (release an item). The example given is transferring dirty laundry into a washing machine, but you'll notice these steps can be used for other similar tasks, such as putting trash in the bin or gathering things off the floor.

TRY THIS

1. Before your first session, introduce your dog to the washing machine and dryer, and make sure they're comfortable with putting their head in or stepping up if it's a top-loading machine. Toss in a few treats or a favorite toy, making it seem normal and fun to fetch them out of the machine.

2. Starting with a basket of laundry, pick up a clothing item and introduce it to your dog. Cue them to "take it" and praise.

3. Next, direct your dog to "bring" an item out of the basket. As your dog picks the item up, lead them toward the washing machine, and using your hand to guide and point, tap the place you want your dog to go while carrying it.

4. When your dog is positioned in the right spot, cue them to "out" or drop the item. Immediately when they drop the item into the washing machine, mark and reward and praise heavily.

5. Use plenty of encouragement through the process. With enough practice, things will click and your dog will understand how they are regrouping the items by transferring each one into the washing machine.

6. Feel free to introduce a special cue or word to the items or locations involved, just keep the cue words consistent. But keep in mind, you don't want to add a cue until a behavior is already happening with some success.

7. To train your dog to retrieve items in the opposite way, out of the dryer and into a laundry basket, use the same process.

Need Help? If your dog is having trouble getting the items to the desired target, start by having them bring the items to your hands, and "out" into your hands. Position your hands closer to the goal each time. If your dog does not release the items once they're in the right spot, spend more time practicing the "out" or "drop it" command.

TASK 2:
ASSISTING WITH CLOTHING REMOVAL

What Does My Dog Need to Learn? For handlers living with mobility limitations, removing items of clothing can be a painful or difficult. Using the skills learned in "retrieve" (see page 48) and "pull" (see page 58) training, a dog can learn to grip and pull on clothing to assist the handler with dressing and undressing. Start with a pair of large, thick socks. Later, you can progress to regular socks, and once your dog is comfortable with that, you can transfer these skills to other items of clothing. In general, start by gathering a bit of slack in the fabric, such as the sleeve of a jacket, and apply the same training as follows to teach your dog to assist in removing other types of clothing. To teach shoe removal, begin with the shoe in your hand. Start by teaching the dog to carefully pull the loose end of the laces, then grip the shoe from the heel area to pull it off.

TRY THIS

1. From a seated position, introduce the item in your hands by placing your hand into the sock about halfway. You'll leave several inches of fabric hanging off your hand for your dog to grab on to. This will also allow your dog to practice and learn to feel out what they're biting, and avoid biting your fingers or toes.

2. Present your sock hand to your dog, and mark and reward for any interaction or touch of it. This will help get your dog interested.

3. Cue "take it" or "pull," and mark and reward successful attempts. This training should be slow and calm. If your dog accidentally bites your fingers, make a sharp noise (such as "ah!" or "ouch!") and take your hand away for a minute. Then try again.

4. After several successful practice sessions with the sock on your hand, practice with the socks on your feet. Place the socks partially on your feet, with several inches of fabric hanging off your toes.

5. Hold your foot slightly up, at a level that is comfortable. Direct your dog to your sock, and cue "take it" or "pull."

6. Put your hand out to take the sock, mark and reward with food, and praise your dog for delivering the sock to your hand.

7. Repeat with the other foot.

8. As you progress in practicing, gradually move the sock higher and snugger on your foot.

? **Need Help?** If your dog doesn't show much interest in putting their mouth on the sock while it's on your hand, wiggle and move it around to get their interest. If your dog struggles with being too rough or biting your fingers through the sock, practice again at a time when they are calmer. It takes practice for your dog to carefully feel out what is okay to grab.

TASK 3:
BRINGING A DRINK FROM THE FRIDGE

What Does My Dog Need to Learn? The steps to bringing a drink from the fridge require a "pull" for doors, a "bring" or retrieve for the drink, and a "touch target" to close the door. Chaining (or linking) behaviors requires a dog to put forth effort. Use plenty of cheerleading and encouragement when the dog is putting in effort.

TRY THIS

1. Keep the drinks in the same location, such as the bottom shelf on the inside of the refrigerator door. Introduce the dog to holding and retrieving the type of bottle you want them to bring (avoid glass during practice in case they drop it). This allows them to get used to the feel and weight of it.

2. As a refresher, practice the "pull it" (see page 58), "bring it" (see page 52), and "touch a target" (see page 60) tasks separately until all are solidly understood and performed by the dog. Then chain them together.

3. Start by going over "pull it" to open the fridge door. Attach your pull handle to the fridge door. Allow your dog to see you doing this.

4. Next, practice retrieves of the drink. Do this while holding the fridge door open or propping it open. Direct your dog to the same area of the fridge, and tap the bottle or can with your finger. You may label this as "drink" when you practice to build item recognition over time.

5. Refresh your dog's skills on "touch target" by propping open the fridge door yourself, standing close enough to direct your dog to show them where to target. Then practice from farther away, sending your dog to close the door.

6. Now you're ready to chain these behaviors together. Go through each command and help your dog along the way as necessary. Then chain them together again. When well-practiced, you can cue your dog to "bring drink," and follow up with praise or reward when they return to close the door.

? **Need Help?** If your dog struggles through any particular step, spend some extra time working on that step by itself. Always encourage your dog to keep at it and to try again. While you are in the process of training this task, you'll want to prevent your dog from opening the fridge when you haven't asked them to. To avoid any bad habits from developing, remove the strap from the door handle when you're not training.

TASK 4:
BRINGING A DOG BOWL AND PLACING IT ON THE COUNTERTOP

What Does My Dog Need to Learn? Dogs love to work for their food. This retrieve has a reward built right in. When your dog brings their food bowl to you, they get dinner. This task is helpful for those who cannot easily bend over to pick up their dog's bowl off the floor. Your dog should already understand "step up," or placing two paws on the counter, before they learn to place items up on a countertop. If they don't yet, spend a little time practicing this. If your dog is not tall enough to reach the counter, or if you prefer, you can have your dog deliver the bowl to your hand. You will need a bowl that is durable, such as one made of stainless steel or silicone. Ceramic bowls are heavy and easily broken.

TRY THIS

1. You don't have to wait until your dog's mealtime to train this task. While training, you may toss a small treat or pieces of kibble (portioned from their regular meals) into your dog's bowl each time they successfully bring it.

2. Place your dog's empty food bowl in its usual spot.

3. Place your dog's food or training treats on the counter near you. Call your dog over to you, shake the food, and in a happy tone of voice, say "Are you hungry?" or some other cue to get them excited for food.

4. Using body language and pointing to direct them to their empty bowl, say "bring bowl" and encourage your dog to pick up the bowl.

5. If they try, but initially drop the bowl, keep your attitude upbeat, keep them on task, and ask them to try again.

6. When your dog delivers the bowl to your hand, mark and reward by placing the treats in the bowl and holding it out for them to eat from.

7. To get your dog to deliver the bowl to the counter, orient yourself to facing the counter as your dog is bringing the bowl, and tap your hand on the counter and indicate your dog to "step up." When they step up (resting their front paws on the counter), use your command for "out" or "drop it" to have them release the bowl onto the counter, rather than taking it into your hand.

Need Help? If your dog drops the bowl, don't pick it up. Ask them again to "bring" until they can deliver it either to your hand, or up onto the counter. When doing retrieves, it's common for a dog to bring the wrong item. Don't scold your dog—simply take the incorrect item with a smile, place it out of the way, then repeat the command for the desired item. If your dog's empty food bowl is identical to their water bowl and they are next to each other, your dog may accidentally retrieve the water bowl. This can create quite a spill. You may want to keep your dog's water bowl in a different location than the food bowl, so it's less likely you'll have a mistake and water spilled. A stainless steel water pail with a handle can be easier to set down than a regular bowl.

TASK 5:
TAKING A RECEIPT FROM A CASHIER AND DELIVERING IT TO A HANDLER

What Does My Dog Need to Learn? If you have physical limitations in reaching or use of hands, or are a wheelchair user, you will find this task helpful. It involves retrieving an item from another person and delivering the item to the handler. It can be modified or adapted for different situations. The prerequisites are a formal retrieve and practicing on items similar to a paper receipt. You may also practice this exercise using a credit card or alternative object of your choice.

TRY THIS

1. You will need a helper to train retrieves with another person. Make sure your helper is someone who your dog is comfortable and confident working with, and ideally, someone who will follow your instructions.

2. Act out the position you'll encounter in real life, such as sitting down or standing with your dog at your side. Have your helper person stand nearby.

3. Take a folded piece of paper, or store receipt paper, and prime your dog by practicing one or two retrieves with just you and your dog. Have your dog retrieve the paper directly from your hand, and briefly hold it, using "take it" and "hold." Mark and reward, and get your dog excited to train.

4. Hand the paper receipt to your helper person, and return to your original position a few feet away.

5. Instruct your helper to hold the receipt extended in their hand, while holding relatively still.

6. Send your dog, using the command "bring."

7. When your dog returns to you with the item, praise heavily and mark and reward.

8. Next, add a table or desk to imitate a counter. Have your helper stand behind the "counter."

9. From the opposite side, send your dog to "bring" the item to you, encouraging them to "step up," with their front paws only, in order to reach the item.

> **?** **Need Help?** If your dog hesitates to "step up" onto the counter, go up to the counter and tap on it, encouraging them up. You may also use the collar and leash to help guide your dog to place their front paws onto the counter.

FOUR
PSYCHIATRIC AND MEDICAL ASSISTANCE TASKS

WHEN IT comes to psychiatric or medical assistance, service dogs are trained to respond to specific commands, events, or triggers to address both urgent and every-day needs. Many tasks have proven vital to the well-being of handlers. This chapter includes psychiatric alerting tasks, such as medicine reminders and room checks, as well as other types of alerting tasks, such as finding a specific person or finding lost items. Some of these tasks will require experimentation to find what works best for you.

84 ALERTING TASKS FOR PSYCHIATRIC CONDITIONS

86 TASK 1: "COVER" OR DEEP PRESSURE THERAPY (DPT)

88 TASK 2: PROVIDING MEDICATION REMINDERS

90 TASK 3: BLOCKING OR CROWD CONTROL

93 TASK 4: ROOM CHECKS

96 TASK 5: INTERRUPTING REPETITIVE BEHAVIORS OR SELF-HARM

98 ALERTING TASKS FOR OTHER MEDICAL CONDITIONS

100 TASK 1: FINDING A PERSON BY NAME

102 TASK 2: FINDING A LOST OR MISPLACED ITEM

104 TASK 3: RETRIEVING AN UNNOTICED DROPPED ITEM

106 TASK 4: WAKING A HANDLER TO AN ALARM

108 TASK 5: WAKING A HANDLER HAVING NIGHT DISTURBANCES

ALERTING TASKS FOR PSYCHIATRIC CONDITIONS

The positive partnership between human and dog is widely known to improve quality of life for those with psychiatric conditions. Particular tasks will vary based on your needs. Aside from formally trained tasks, a dog can help stabilize your daily routine, boost confidence, and provide needed companionship. You may even choose to teach your dog extra tasks, like retrieving objects or opening doors, just for the sake of it. Things you can do on your own (such as picking up an object) would not count toward the legal requirement of tasks, but they can still add to your dog's training and provide things to work on together.

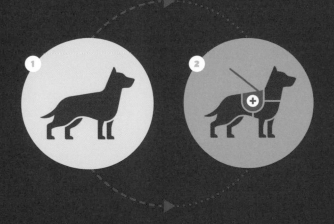

MEDICAL ALERT
AND RESPONSE

PSYCHIATRIC

TASK 1:
"COVER" OR DEEP PRESSURE THERAPY (DPT)

What Does My Dog Need to Learn? Your dog will learn to lie across an area of your body on a cue, such as lying across the chest, abdomen, or lap. The dog's weight and warmth provide calming pressure and a grounding effect, and may help slow breathing and heart rate. Some handlers use this task during a panic attack, dissociative episode, flashback, or sensory overload. Others use it for conditions that involve muscular or nerve pain. The pressure can be a distraction from pain in other areas of the body. Working with a dog that naturally seeks human contact makes DPT much easier. The exact way you teach DPT depends on your lifestyle and what works best for you. Some find certain pressure points work best. Practice to find an amount of pressure that is therapeutic and tolerable.

TRY THIS

1. Get in a comfortable position, either sitting on the floor or lying down.

2. Using a treat as a lure in your hand, guide your dog up and over you, until they are standing above your lap or the area of your body you want pressure on. Praise and give a treat before you release your dog. Practice this until your dog is comfortable stepping and standing over you.

3. Next, lower your treat hand, and encourage them to lie down on top of you, luring into a position that works best for you. When your dog is in the desired position, calmly praise and give them the treat.

4. Continually praise while the dog holds the position you want and settles into it with their full weight. This is a calm exercise, so keep praise low-key.

5. Add a cue, such as "cover." If you want to teach a second position, label them separately with different cues.

6. From a seated position, you can teach your large dog to do DPT with only their front feet and elbows on you and their back feet on the floor. Give this position a different cue, such as "hug" or "cuddle."

7. To teach front feet only, tap on your lap, asking them to come up, then mark and reward when they are in the right position.

8. Finish each session with an "off" cue, guiding your dog off you using a food lure or leash and collar guidance.

Need Help? If your dog pops up out of a down position as you're luring or rewarding, make sure you keep the reward low, between their front paws. Use the lure and food rewards to teach short-duration positioning. Gradually add a minute or so each time you practice. Try to fade the food rewards fairly soon, and emphasize praise and affection as rewards.

TASK 2:
PROVIDING MEDICATION REMINDERS

What Does My Dog Need to Learn? Training a dog to remind their handler to take medication depends on the dog's internal clock, as well as other context clues. Medication alerts are paired with the dog getting reinforcement with a treat or walk. A dog should be encouraged to repeat a cue, becoming increasingly pushy, until the handler gets up and takes their medication, followed by the dog getting a special treat. Be aware that this task can take a long time to build reliability. It is helpful if you have a highly motivated dog. This task can also be modified for any daily routine reminders.

TRY THIS

1. Pushy behavior should be encouraged for this task. You may teach your dog to alert you with a paw-touch (see page 62), nose-push (see page 32), or another cue you will recognize and respond to.

2. Start by setting alarms on your phone for each time you will take your medication, or use an app designed to do such.

The alarm will serve as a cue for your dog, and have a positive association with action and reward.

3. When the alarm goes off, encourage your dog to "touch" or nudge you. Once they have persisted for long enough (as you shape it), mark with a "yes" or click, and get up and move toward where you'd normally take your medication.

4. Keep your medication in a location along with a hard container of high-value treats.

5. Each time you get up and go take your medication, follow it by giving your dog a special treat.

6. Alternatively, pair the medication reminder with a non-food reward, such as a walk, a trip outside, or a game with a toy. Keep it connected to the behavior by rewarding your dog each time after you take your medication.

7. To transition from setting an alarm to your dog alerting on their own takes time. To capture and reward a response with no alarm, try setting your alarm slightly later (assuming it's safe for you to do so), such as 15 to 30 minutes later than you were practicing. See if your dog starts to recognize it's time even without the alarm, and if so, reward big-time. In some cases, a dog will also develop the perception of when their human needs medication. This is often based on the dog's ability to detect subtle physical signs.

8. Keep in mind dogs are not robots, so any time your dog alerts, always double-check that it's the right time. If your dog gives you false alerts at a time that's way off, don't reward that. Redirect your dog to something else, then wait until they're within at least 30 minutes of accuracy to reward.

? **Need Help?** If you need more of a reminder, it may be helpful to teach your dog to bring medication to you at certain times, such as when an alarm sounds or when you wake up or go to bed. It may take a while to train, but eventually your dog will bring meds at the right time, on their own.

TASK 3:
BLOCKING OR CROWD CONTROL

What Does My Dog Need to Learn? A block is a preventative task that puts a buffer of space between the handler and crowds. It is essentially a positioning exercise with a built-in stay. The dog is taught to circle the handler, and stay in a standing position in front of or behind them as a buffer, so that people in public won't bump into them or come too close. It can be helpful for proximity sensitivities, as well as some medical disorders in which a bump or touch can elicit severe pain. This task is not for everybody. Some people find that this task helps them greatly, prevents possibly triggering events, and gives them a feeling of "watching my back." But for others it can become a hindrance in their development of better coping skills. Consider how it fits in with your long-term plan. Throughout this task, the dog should remain calm and neutral to strangers. Keep in mind service dogs should never behave aggressively or nervously around strangers.

TRY THIS

1. It is helpful if your dog knows a "stand-stay" command. You will keep them standing for blocking. When a dog is standing, they are more visible and less prone to have a paw or tail stepped on or run over with a cart.

2. As you stand stationary, practice directing your dog in a complete circle around your body. Do this using a treat lure, leash guidance, or a combination of both. It is helpful to have a treat in each hand while luring a full circle. If the leash is cumbersome at first, switch to a short-tab (see page 17) or practice without a leash while you're using the food lures.

3. Keep your dog close to your body. Some handlers prefer the dog to stand close enough to be touching them. It can be helpful to practice against a wall or in a tight area so your dog gets comfortable orbiting around you closely.

4. Introduce the cue "in back" as you direct your dog to stand behind you, perpendicular to your back. Mark and reward when they are in the desired position.

5. Continue to reward your dog for staying in the desired position.

6. As you practice, begin to fade the lure, and just use your empty hand to direct your dog. Mark and reward when they get into the correct position.

7. Using a helper person, act out the real-life situations of someone coming up behind you, in front of you, or next to you.

8. As the person approaches and stops behind you or in front of you, direct your dog to the position you want, between you and the person, or behind you with the cue "in back."

9. During this task, your dog should be neutral to the helpers or strangers and not fixated on them. Make sure to look back often to see how your dog is doing. Reward your dog for holding the position and for focusing on you.

10. To end the exercise, cue your dog back to regular heel position, or release your dog with a cue such as "free" or "all done."

? **Need Help?** If your dog is not reliably holding the stand-stay position, spend some time refreshing basic obedience and working on stand-stays. Practice having your dog move from a "sit" or "down" to a "stand."

TASK 4:
ROOM CHECKS

What Does My Dog Need to Learn? For this task, the dog learns to check rooms inside the home, letting the handler know the room is clear and there's nobody unexpected in it. It's intended to provide a sense of security and a reality check to handlers coping with a variety of conditions, such as PTSD, flashbacks, or hallucinations. This is not an actual security dog task, and the dog is never encouraged to respond aggressively to a threat. It is meant to give the handler a sense of safety and increased well-being. Your dog will learn to go into a room they're directed into, cover the room and make sure all is normal, and return to the handler. You can also teach your dog to alert with a bark if they find someone in the room, which will require your dog to already understand a "speak" cue.

TRY THIS

1. Choose a room you will use for practice.

2. Start with your dog on-leash. Open the door, and take your dog through the pattern of the perimeter of the room. Moving from left to right, walk past all four corners of the room.

3. Next, go into the room when your dog isn't looking, and place a treat in each of the four corners of the room. You may also include closets, if needed.

4. With your dog still on-leash, say "go check" and walk the same pattern, pausing at each corner, and directing your dog to go get the treats.

5. Once you have repeated this a few times, send your dog into the room on their own and cue "go check" while you wait at the doorway. While your dog is still learning the exercise, keep laying out a treat in all four corners of the room ahead of time.

6. After your dog has had enough time to check the room, call them back to you.

7. As you continue to practice, vary the number of treats in the room, so there's anywhere from one to four in the room in different corners.

8. Generalize by practicing in any other rooms you'd plan to have the dog check, and don't forget to practice with lights off.

9. Optionally, teach your dog to indicate if there is someone in the room. You will need a helper person. Make sure your dog is totally comfortable interacting with any helpers you use.

10. Begin outside the room by handing your helper person a treat or toy to use as a reward.

11. Have your helper person in the room with treat rewards ready. Your helper will cue the dog to "speak" when they find them.

12. Send your dog into the room with the cue "go check."

13. When your dog alerts with a bark and is rewarded by the helper, immediately call your dog back to you and mark and reward.

14. Repeat until the dog barks at the helper without having to be cued by them. They should reward them every time. Remember to only allow one bark, then call your dog back and reward.

15. Praise the dog each time they check a room, and refresh the training with a helper person every so often.

Need Help? A dog may begin to lose interest in the room checks task over time. To maintain your dog's long-term motivation, put treats in the corners of the room for your dog to find every so often. Your dog will never know when a reward is expected and will keep trying. If your dog struggles to "speak" or bark on cue with the helper person, spend some time teaching the cue at home yourself. When you practice this on your own, limit it to just a few repetitions, and only allow barking when it's been cued with the command.

TASK 5:
INTERRUPTING REPETITIVE BEHAVIORS OR SELF-HARM

What Does My Dog Need to Learn? Repetitive or self-harm behaviors can be things like skin picking, OCD rituals, stimming, skin biting, trichotillomania (hair pulling), and similar, and a dog can be trained to interrupt such behavior. Interrupting self-harm is not a verbally cued behavior. The dog learns to read the handler's physical cues and respond appropriately. To train a response to an action when it actually happens, the behavior has to be acted out in training sessions and repeated consistently until the dog can recognize the cues and respond appropriately. Try to shape an alert that can help you become aware of what you are doing or that will redirect your focus to your dog. Note that training interruption of any behaviors involving sharp or dangerous objects is risky to both the dog and handler and should be avoided.

TRY THIS

1. Know the behavior you want your dog to interrupt (this depends on the individual and their condition and symptoms) and the type of alert you want. Some alert behaviors you might encourage are nose-push, paw-tap, step up with front paws on your lap, or initiating DPT/cover (see page 86). Find a combination of what your dog does readily and what will work for you, making sure it's an alert you won't easily ignore.

2. Act out the behaviors, then reward your dog to create an association. In this step, you're not looking for an alert or behavior from the dog. You're simply associating it with food to teach the dog that it is relevant to pay attention to. Repeat this over a period of time, until you notice the dog begins to expect a treat when they see the behavior.

3. Add an alert or interruption. Act out the behavior and cue your dog to do a behavior that will interrupt it. You will phase out this verbal or signal cue quickly, as the dog's cue will be the physical signs of the behavior itself.

4. When your dog alerts as desired, or does a task that interrupts you, mark and heavily reward and praise.

5. Use your dog's alerts as a cue to become more aware of your behavior and to interrupt and help you stop the behavior.

6. Petting, attention, a walk, or games with a toy are all good rewards to try. Interactive activities can redirect handler behavior.

? **Need Help?** If you want your dog to target a certain part of your body when alerting and they're off, try shaping the behavior by waiting to mark and reward until they're alerting closer to the area you want. Don't allow barking, as this is not a suitable alert in public places.

ALERTING TASKS FOR OTHER MEDICAL CONDITIONS

All alerting uses some kind of cue the dog senses—sight, sound, scent, or otherwise. Our first goal for medical alerts is to get the dog to realize that cues or events are meaningful, because they are associated with rewards. Then the cue is paired with a trained alert from the dog. In this section, we will go over how to train your dog to find people or lost items or wake you up, be it from an alarm or a nightmare. Many of these tasks are helpful to those who have trouble thinking clearly due to medication side effects or those with memory loss, traumatic brain injuries, or other conditions.

MEDICAL ALERT AND RESPONSE

PSYCHIATRIC

TASK 1:
FINDING A PERSON BY NAME

What Does My Dog Need to Learn? The behavior of finding a person by name can be used in a variety of different situations. This behavior takes time and practice. Keep your long-term goals in mind by planning ahead for shaping the most useful tasks for your needs. There are different ways this task can be used. At home, the dog can get help for a handler who is unable to call for help. For this task, the helper person should follow the dog back to the handler. This exercise is also needed for two other tasks: retrieving an item and bringing it to a named person and guiding a handler to a specific person.

TRY THIS

1. Begin this exercise at home with your helper person in another room nearby. They should be out of sight but within hearing distance so they can hear when you send your dog.

2. Verbally cue your dog to "Go find [name]." If you use hand signals, you may also point to direct your dog to go.

100 Service Dog Training Guide

3. After your helper person hears your "go find" cue, they should call your dog using the dog's name and an encouraging but informal cue such as "Pup, pup, pup!"

4. When your dog reaches the helper, the helper rewards the dog with a piece of food and praise. For now, the only time the dog receives food rewards from the helper person is after the dog has been specifically sent by the handler.

5. Encourage your dog to return to you. The helper should follow your dog back to you.

6. When your dog returns with the helper person, heavily praise and reward your dog. Associate the name again, saying "Good job! Find [name]."

7. Practice from different rooms and increasing distances, gradually fading the helper's verbal encouragement, until the dog can find the helper person with no assistance.

8. This task is best done within the home or a safe contained environment. It is not generally safe for your dog to be off-leash out of your sight to search for someone in public. When teaching searching for someone in public, the dog will not leave the handler and will guide them on-lead.

? **Need Help?** If your dog is hesitant to leave you even when the other person calls to encourage them, start the game with your helper closer. Then gradually increase the distance. If you have multiple people in the home and your dog goes to the wrong person (not the one you've named), decide if you want to be specific or if it's just as useful for your dog to find anyone within the home. If you want to be specific, anyone the dog goes to who is not calling the dog should ignore the dog.

TASK 2:
FINDING A LOST OR MISPLACED ITEM

What Does My Dog Need to Learn? Your dog will learn how to find a misplaced item and bring it to you. This task requires thorough practice, and your dog must have a solid retrieve command (see page 52) and plenty of practice retrieving the specific item you will be teaching your dog to search for and find (in this example, keys). If you want your dog to be able to find the item on tables and counters, practice retrieving it from these places before beginning. If you want to train the dog to retrieve a phone, it's best to train retrieval from a single location where they can always find it, such as a cordless phone that is always on the same low table or placed on the floor.

TRY THIS

1. Outfit your set of keys with a special keychain, attaching something that makes it easier for your dog to find and carry the keys. A short length of leather or knotted fabric works well.

2. If you choose to, you may also scent the keychain with a specific odor that your dog will learn to associate with the specific item, making it easier to find. You can use a drop of clove oil, birch oil, or any dog-safe essential oil. (Note that odors dissipate over time and will need to be refreshed every so often.)

3. Make sure you've practiced retrieves of the keys from different locations, giving your dog tons of praise when they bring you the keys. You may also use food rewards, or toy rewards.

4. Now you're going to place the keys in a new location (without your dog seeing). Choose an easy location you've previously done retrieves in, like on a chair or somewhere in plain sight. Start with easy finds, near your dog's eye level.

5. Invite your dog back into the room, and cue "find keys."

6. Next, hide the keys in the same place and cover them with a hand towel or something else your dog can nudge away.

7. Encourage your dog to nudge into the towel to find and take the keys.

8. Repeat in various places that keys might be commonly lost, such as your purse or backpack, jacket pocket, desk, floor, between couch cushions, etc.

Need Help? Dogs often learn by trial and error. If your dog brings you the incorrect item, thank your dog, but don't give them a reward. Cue the behavior again, encouraging your dog to try again until they get it right. It is important that your dog has the motivation to keep trying. If your dog needs more motivation, try playing with them with a plush keychain or braided/knotted fabric.

TASK 3:
RETRIEVING AN UNNOTICED DROPPED ITEM

What Does My Dog Need to Learn? Using your choice of retrieve items, the dog will learn to automatically retrieve a dropped item when the handler is not looking. This task is beneficial to someone who may not notice or hear that they dropped an essential item. We will act out a situation where we drop something without knowing it.

TRY THIS

1. Choose an item your dog enjoys retrieving and has retrieved many times successfully before (on cue). Try to pick something that you can subtly place under your arm or in your pocket, so you can "accidentally" drop it without the dog seeing it ahead of time.

2. Start by busying yourself doing something, then "unexpectedly" drop the item, and see what your dog does.

3. If your dog automatically picks it up, make a huge deal of it and praise and reward.

4. If your dog does not automatically pick it up, stop what you're doing and look around like you aren't sure where the item went. This may cue your dog to recognize something was dropped.

5. If your dog needs more direction to get it, bring their attention to the item by making it move if you can. Then cue them to "bring" while gesturing to the dropped object.

6. Encourage your dog to come around to your front once they have the object.

7. Over time, practice with other items.

? **Need Help?** Don't be surprised if your dog tries to bring you things you left on the floor on purpose, now that they know it's fun to be a helper! Now is a good time to refresh "leave it" by giving the command, followed by dropping something. This way, if you accidentally drop something that you don't want your dog to pick up, like food or a sharp object, your "leave it" will stop your dog before they pick up anything they shouldn't.

TASK 4:
WAKING A HANDLER TO AN ALARM

What Does My Dog Need to Learn? Your dog will learn to respond to the sound of an alarm and prompt you to wake up through tactile stimulation, nose-nudging, or a pawing alert. Hearing-related tasks require a dog to recognize an alarm and learn persistence in alerting. It's best to use a phone that can have various alarms set as you practice and pretend to be asleep. When the alarm sounds, the dog should push at the handler and persistently alert until they get up and reward the dog. Each dog has its own individual way of alerting that can be recognized and shaped to be most effective.

TRY THIS

1. Begin by associating the sound of the alarm with action and treats. This is to build the dog's excitement for the sound. Alarm noise means get up on the bed and treats!

2. Lie in bed with your dog near you and a pouch of treats. Later you can keep the treats in a sealed container next to where the alarm is.

3. Set an alarm to go off at intervals of every minute or less.

4. When the alarm goes off, reward the dog with food by simply grabbing a few treats and quickly tossing them next to you in bed.

5. With your alarms set at one-minute intervals or less, lie back down, pretending to sleep.

6. This time, don't react or respond to the alarm. Wait for your dog to make some sort of physical contact with you on their own.

7. When they make any contact with you, immediately mark and reward.

8. Continue to pretend to sleep and mark and reward any type of contact your dog makes to alert you.

9. Next, practice ignoring your dog's alerts to make sure they will continue to push and alert until they're successful in waking you. Raise the criteria by not responding to the alarm, or to your dog's first alert. Wait for them to alert or touch you a second time, and a third time, until the alert is enough to wake you from even a deep sleep.

10. Once they persist, sit up and praise them enthusiastically. Make sure to turn the alarm off once they respond by waking you.

? **Need Help?** Sometimes the alert behaviors we expect aren't the ones the dog wants to give naturally. See what behaviors are most natural for your dog. Always praise persistence and be observant of your dog's natural abilities to communicate. A huge part of building alerts is the relationship.

TASK 5:
WAKING A HANDLER HAVING NIGHT DISTURBANCES

What Does My Dog Need to Learn? Night terrors, nightmares, and disruptive sleep can be interrupted by a service dog performing "cover" or deep pressure therapy over a handler's body (see page 86), so they'll need that skill first. Because some sleep disturbances can cause thrashing around and movement, this may not be advisable for a smaller dog. Alternatively, the dog may be taught to lick the handler's face to wake them. Feel free to substitute the type of alert you want.

TRY THIS

1. In order to train a dog to respond to a sleep event, you will act out the event. You need to know what your movements and sounds look like. This can be accomplished by video recording a night's sleep in which you have an episode.

2. Let's say the sleep disturbance is characterized by vocalizing and leg movement. Start training by acting out those

behaviors and associating the event with a reward. This makes it relevant to your dog. Think of it like an introduction. This will also help assure your movements or sounds aren't frightening to your dog.

3. Lie in bed, along with the food rewards you'll be using to condition the association. Lie quietly for at least 10 seconds. Act out the event for 5 to 10 seconds. Follow it immediately with delivering a reward to the dog.

4. Next, act out the event for about 10 seconds, then guide your dog to the position or cue you want. If it's "cover" across the abdomen, lure your dog into the position and mark and reward. Spend some time calmly praising your dog in the "cover" position before releasing your dog with an "off" command.

5. Start each repetition with the dog near the bed but not immediately next to you.

6. Practice until your dog understands to automatically "cover" on you when you act out the sleep behaviors.

? Need Help? When practicing, try to train for response only after at least five seconds or more, as you don't want your dog feeling the need to assist you any time you're simply tossing and turning in regular sleep.

FIVE
MOBILITY SUPPORT TASKS

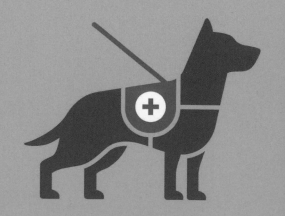

MOBILITY SUPPORT dogs help people who are limited in their physical abilities—such as those with limited range of motion, strength, or balance—move, regain stability on their own, and accomplish day-to-day tasks. In earlier chapters, we covered light mobility tasks involving retrieves (see page 52) and daily living assistance (see page 68). This chapter covers additional tasks that involve guiding, alerting, or assisting handlers through specific environments and situations, as well as some general information about mobility training. Mobility dogs often perform a combination of tasks based on the individual needs of the handler.

112 GUIDING TASKS

114 TASK 1: LEADING FORWARD ON CUE

116 TASK 2: TAKING ME TO AN EXIT OR OUTSIDE

118 TASK 3: FOLLOWING ANOTHER PERSON

120 TASK 4: ALERTING A HANDLER TO STEPS OR CHANGES IN ELEVATION

122 TASK 5: FINDING A SEAT

124 WEIGHT-BEARING MOBILITY TRAINING AND TASKS

128 TASK 1: MOVING FROM SITTING TO STANDING

130 TASK 2: PROVIDING BALANCE ON STAIRS

132 TASK 3: BRACING AN UNSTABLE HANDLER

GUIDING TASKS

Contrary to popular belief, a guide dog doesn't know where to go until they're directed. Training a guide dog for helping someone with vision impairment is a highly specialized process, and we won't delve into training a guide dog in this book. That being said, some types of guiding can be useful for other disabilities and situations, particularly those involving mobility or conditions that cause faintness, weakness, dizziness, disorientation, or panic. This could be anything from diabetes to medication side effects, and many of these tasks help handlers find a safe place to rest or exit.

TASK 1:
LEADING FORWARD ON CUE

What Does My Dog Need to Learn? This is foundational work before teaching tasks like "take me to an exit" (see page 116) or "follow another person" (see page 118). Your dog should already know heel position and be able to perform heeling on-leash through basic to advanced obedience training. Although proper heeling means the dog is never leading or straining on the leash, by using a harness or different cues, you can teach your dog to guide you forward on command. While you can teach this on a collar and leash, it's best to train with a harness designed for light mobility (see page 125). This way, the feeling of leading ahead will be light pressure against the harness, and the dog will not learn to pull when on their normal collar and leash. The goal is to teach the dog to guide you lightly ahead, at the correct pace for you to follow without being pulled.

TRY THIS

1. Start with the right equipment. You'll need your regular collar and leash. If your dog has a properly fitted harness with a handle you may use that, but if that's not long

enough or comfortable, have a second leash attached to the harness for this exercise.

2. Make sure your dog has been introduced to wearing the harness. Do this by having them wear it for a few minutes in the house each day, and if they're doing well with it, add short walks in the harness until they're comfortable.

3. To introduce the "go forward" exercise, the dog needs a target to reach. A target can be anything visible that you will bait with a treat, such as a Frisbee or plastic plate.

4. With your dog at heel position next to your side, leave them at a stay.

5. Set out your target on the floor a distance away, but close enough that your dog can see it. About 20 feet is good to start, and you can increase distance as you practice.

6. Bait the target with a treat.

7. Return to your dog, and while holding the leash attached to the harness (or harness handle if your dog is tall enough), position yourself slightly behind your dog (about one to two feet) and encourage them to go toward the target. Use verbal encouragement such as "go get it" and body language, praising as they move forward ahead of you. You are not introducing a verbal command of "go forward" yet.

8. Repeat steps 4 through 7 while making sure your dog stays at a pace that is comfortable for you to follow. The exact position and pace will depend on your work as a team.

9. To end the exercise, direct your dog back to heel and enforce the position with the leash and collar.

? **Need Help?** If your dog lurches ahead and pulls too quickly, don't allow them to reach the target—stop immediately each time they pull too hard. Go back to the distance you began at, and try again. Move slower so they understand the speed and light pressure felt through the harness.

TASK 2:
TAKING ME TO AN EXIT OR OUTSIDE

What Does My Dog Need to Learn? You can begin teaching your dog to lead you outside or to an exit once you've taught them how to confidently lead forward on cue. Leading to an exit can be useful for those who need to leave a situation due to rising anxiety, symptoms of PTSD, or disorientation. However, it's important to only use this task if it's safe for you to do so, and if it will benefit you overall rather than hinder your progress in learning to cope with situations by staying in them. If you are having a medical episode or panic attack, it's often safest to stop where you are and look for somewhere to sit down until you've recovered and it's safe for you to walk around.

TRY THIS

1. Begin this exercise at home, with your dog in the proper equipment for forward guiding.

2. Start with one door to the outside. Place your target several feet outside the door, and bait it with a treat.

3. In the beginning, allow your dog to see you bait the target. Now it is in their mind.

4. Choose a cue word that's different than the word you use for your regular trips. You may not want to say "outside" if your dog associates that with a walk or potty break.

5. From inside the home, cue your dog to "exit," and encourage them to lead you to the door.

6. Once you both go through the door to outside, praise your dog heavily and allow them to eat the treat off the target.

7. Repeat, starting farther away.

8. When your dog is getting the idea of what "exit" means, it's time to phase out the target and treat, and begin generalizing on different exit doors, and in different buildings.

9. To introduce your dog to "exit" in a new place, such as a large store, don't wait until you're already toward the back of the store. Practice an easier "exit" first, soon after entering.

10. Once you've phased out the target, use praise and a treat when your dog takes you through the door without the target.

11. Use the times you regularly leave a building or the home. Each time you walk out the door, say "exit" simply to associate the word, so your dog understands this means going outside.

12. Do not allow your dog to lead or guide you unless you direct them to. Otherwise, keep your dog heeling next to you.

Need Help? If your dog gets confused or doesn't go toward the door when practicing, start closer and allow them to see the target outside. Some dogs may get confused in larger public places and end up taking you to the elevator or bathrooms. Try to practice in the places you most frequently go, so your dog learns the layout. Remember, if at any point you become disoriented and it's unsafe for you to be walking around (even if guided by your dog), please stop and find somewhere to sit down so you're both safe.

TASK 3:
FOLLOWING ANOTHER PERSON

What Does My Dog Need to Learn? Teach your dog to follow a helper person, such as a friend leading you through a crowd, a restaurant host, or an employee taking you to a certain area of a store. As your dog follows, they will be slightly ahead of you and guiding you, but still under your control. This can be taught in baby steps. Your dog should already understand "go forward" and how to guide you forward in a straight line or to a target (see page 114).

TRY THIS

1. You will need a helper person who can follow your instructions.

2. With your dog on your left side, stand a few feet behind the helper person.

3. Using your right hand, tap the person on the shoulder to show your dog who they'll be following.

4. Have the helper person hold the dog's leash while you hold the harness (or the leash on the harness) and move forward in tandem.

5. You may also have the helper use treats to reward the dog for following, although this should be phased out quickly once the dog is getting the hang of it.

6. Using your cues of "go forward" and introducing the cue "follow," begin to walk, encouraging your dog to keep going and "follow" the person leading you.

7. Start with just a few steps at a time. Take a few steps, then reward your dog. Take a few more, and reward your dog.

8. As you progress, it's useful to have a landmark or point of distance in mind as a goal with each practice exercise, so the training is as realistic of a setup as possible.

9. Practice moving together through left and right turns, and stopping when the helper person stops ahead of you.

10. Now begin to practice without the helper person holding the leash or having treats. The helper can give a pat or some cue to keep the dog's attention as you direct them to "follow."

11. When you arrive at the point of distance you were aiming for, stop, praise your dog, and have them come back into heel position.

12. Practice with new helper people and also through crowds.

> **?** **Need Help?** If your dog struggles to follow the helper, go back to having the helper hold the leash as you hold your dog leashed by their harness or by the handle. Never allow your dog to solicit attention from strangers or follow people when you haven't directed your dog to "follow."

TASK 4:
ALERTING A HANDLER TO STEPS OR CHANGES IN ELEVATION

What Does My Dog Need to Learn? Some handlers may not notice changes in elevation or steps, and this can present a hazard for them when navigating in public. This exercise will help you teach your dog to alert you to elevation changes by pausing at each curb, step, or drop-off, and only going forward when given the cue to continue to "go forward" (see page 114).

TRY THIS

1. In order to alert or signal to elevation changes or steps, a dog must be working in a position slightly ahead of the handler. The handler must also pay good attention to the dog's signs.

2. When training this, a helper person will be necessary if the handler isn't always noticing the changes in elevation themselves.

3. Using a light mobility guide harness or other harness, refresh your dog's skills by practicing the cue "go forward."

4. Begin by scoping out a good training area for this exercise. Somewhere with clear curbs or one-step elevation changes will work, as you will need to practice many times.

5. As you approach the curb, have your dog stop when they come to it, with just their front paws up on it.

6. Each time you stop on the step up to the curb, mark and reward your dog. Your dog has now begun to associate stopping at each curb with getting a reward.

7. For the down-step off a curb or ledge, teach the dog to stop at the drop-off. Each time you enforce the stop at the curb or at a step, praise and reward your dog.

8. This takes lots of practice, and the handler needs to notice changes in elevation in order to consistently practice and reward the dog.

Need Help? Again, this takes lots of practice. You can associate it with wearing the harness or service dog gear, because your dog may not need to do this when they're off duty. If your dog misses a step or change in elevation, give a verbal correction, back up, and do the step over again, praising them for getting it right on their second try.

TASK 5:
FINDING A SEAT

What Does My Dog Need to Learn? A service dog can be trained to help guide you to a place where you can sit down safely. This task is a combination of guiding and finding or searching, using object discrimination. Your dog will learn to scan the environment and locate a place to sit down, such as a bench, chair, or ledge. As you practice, your dog can generalize to more seating areas. Dogs can come up with smart and creative ways to problem-solve. A prerequisite is the "go forward" command with a target (see page 114). Some handlers find that with practice, their dogs begin to read signs independently and find ways to alert them to when it's time to sit down.

TRY THIS

1. Start at home or in an environment you frequently train in with your training gear on.

2. Introduce the exercise by making an association with reward. Using your target (a Frisbee or plate your dog can see), place it on a chair and bait it.

3. With your dog at your left side at heel position, cue them to guide you forward and to the target.

4. Once they readily take you to the target on the chair, it's time to phase out the target.

5. Next, keeping the same chair in the same position, cue your dog to "find a seat" and praise them as they lead you to the chair.

6. As soon as your dog gets to the chair, mark and reward your dog.

7. Repeat this process, and add sitting down on the chair and praising your dog.

8. Cue your dog "find a seat" from increasingly farther away.

9. Set up exercises at home. A garage or spare room works well. In advance, set up a chair or bench along a wall with other objects in the room. Then walk your dog into the room and cue them to "find a seat." Mark and reward when they lead you to the open seat.

10. You can further strengthen the association by naming it each time you sit down throughout the day, or in a public place. Before you sit on a chair or bench, pat the bench with your hand and say "find a seat" then sit down as normal and praise your dog.

11. You will need to practice in many areas and situations, so as you're out and about, keep an eye out for new places where you can practice this task. If you see a place where there's a different type of bench or chair, use that as an opportunity to help your dog generalize.

Need Help? If your dog seems confused, go back to baiting the seat by placing a treat on it in advance, or have a helper do so. Dogs take time to generalize. If your dog guides you to a seat that is unsuitable for whatever reason, or not quite an actual sitting area but similar, still praise them for trying, especially in the beginning. Then take a few steps away and try again. If they indicate the wrong thing, use your "try again" cue, and give them some help to learn which seats are the type you're looking for.

WEIGHT-BEARING MOBILITY TRAINING AND TASKS

The term "mobility" can include dogs who help with common tasks like retrieving items and opening or closing tasks for a handler with limited function. It also refers to dogs who perform tasks to help physically move or support someone's body. This chapter will focus on tasks involving physical help for the handler's body.

It's a common misconception that dogs can serve as a cane or walker for those with ambulatory issues. They cannot replace mobility aids in all cases. When it comes to weight-bearing mobility tasks involving helping a person move, walk, or balance, there are limits to what a dog can safely do. Dogs are not built like horses, and they simply aren't structured to be weight-bearing animals. Using a dog improperly for mobility can lead to severe injury to the dog or to the handler. Weight-bearing mobility dogs, when properly selected and trained, require a lot of foundational work that includes synchronized movement with the handler. Every handler moves differently, so this work is highly individualized. Here are a few things to consider if you require a service dog that can perform weight-bearing tasks:

Type of Assistance Needed. The first step is determining what type of mobility the handler wants and what is feasible for the dog to do. If every step needs support (other than light steadying or counterbalance with a handle), another mobility aid should be considered, such as a cane or walker. Check page 125 for more on different types of mobility assistance.

Breed, Build, and Age. A dog that does weight-bearing tasks must be a certain size and build to safely work. The breed, as discussed in chapter 1 (see page 7), is also a factor. The dog must be fully grown (growth plates closed), which takes an average of two years but varies by breed. Putting any extra weight on a puppy's unfused joints can cause serious harm.

Mobility dogs should be examined and x-rayed around two years of age by an orthopedic vet prior to beginning any weight-bearing training. A dog's size requirements vary based on the handler's disabilities and needs, but in general, a dog needs to be at least half the handler's weight to do mobility work.

Special Health Considerations. A weight-bearing dog needs special health checks before training. Radiographs of the hips, elbows, spine, and overall structure should be examined by an orthopedic vet prior to beginning training—X-rays alone are not always enough. For example, a dog with hip dysplasia can struggle over time to comfortably support their own weight and should not be taking on extra weight. (Consider obtaining a dog from a breeder who certifies all their breeding dogs' hips and elbows through an organization like OFA or PennHIP.) Most mobility dogs get extra physical conditioning exercises as well as veterinary chiropractic care. It's important that a large dog be kept in good physical condition and never allowed to become overweight. Brace and mobility dogs wear specialized gear, usually a specially fitted harness.

COMMON TYPES OF MOBILITY WORK

Mobility issues come in a variety of forms and require different types of assistance from service dogs. To give you some idea of this range, let's take a quick look at some different types of mobility work:

Light Mobility. These types of tasks include guiding and light pulling, which is any forward motion that results in light pressure against the dog's harness. A long rigid handle is most often used for guide work. Generally, a dog that does light mobility tasks should be at least 30 percent of the handler's height and weight.

Moderate Mobility. These tasks include steadying tasks, in which the dog occasionally provides steadying to a handler with a gait deficit, and counterbalance tasks, in which the dog is trained to provide a point of stability to the handler. These dogs typically wear a specially fitted harness with a semirigid handle that the handler uses for steadiness—not to bear down on—when completing transfers or walking short distances with assistance. To work together and move as a team, the dog must learn to act intuitively to counter the handler's imbalances. They do not perform under command only, but in a fluid partnership with the handler. This requires a lot of practice and knowledgeable instruction. Counterbalance tasks do not involve bracing or putting weight directly onto the dog. Moderate mobility dogs may also train for forward-momentum pulling—pulling forward with their weight to help a handler get up out of a chair, for example—and a harness with a soft handle is most often used. Dogs should never be trained to pull by their collar. Dogs can be trained to safely pull forward in a proper harness quite easily. The frequency with which the dog is expected to do this task should also be taken into account when considering what's safe for the dog.

Moderate to Heavy Mobility. Bracing is considered moderate to heavy mobility. Dogs may be trained for bracing tasks, which require the dog to stand-stay and lock up, allowing the handler to use downward pressure for balance while the dog is still. A bracing harness is used to distribute weight across and over the dog's shoulders, the safest place for a dog to bear any downward weight. Bracing should never be done in motion, on an uneven surface, or when the dog's four feet are not all in correct even position. Bracing is hard on a dog's body and unsuitable for some dogs. Generally, a moderate mobility dog must be more than 50 percent of the handler's height and weight. For heavier tasks, such as bracing for balance or helping a handler get up from the ground, a dog should weigh up to 65 percent of the handler's weight.

Heavy Mobility. This type of work is not appropriate for most dogs! It may require momentum pulls of significant handler weight or a wheelchair. The right dog may be trained to pull a wheelchair up a ramp, but it depends on the physical abilities of the dog, as well as how frequently they will be expected to do the task. Miniature horses are also used for heavier mobility and pulling work.

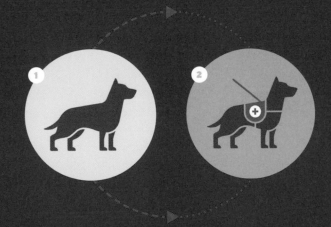

TASK 1:
MOVING FROM SITTING TO STANDING

What Does My Dog Need to Learn? Your dog will learn to help you get from a seated position to a standing one, which requires counterbalance and pulling. This work requires your dog to be able to pull forward against pressure in a harness. Your dog must be fully grown and physically sound. Make sure your dog is capable of safely pulling the amount of weight you expect.

TRY THIS

1. You will need a properly fitted harness with a soft handle that can angle back toward your dog's tail facing you.

2. From a seated position, have your dog in a position within reaching distance and facing away from you.

3. Move as far forward or out of the chair as you are able to on your own.

4. Take hold of the pull handle on your dog's harness, and encourage your dog to pull using the cue "go forward."

5. Use the momentum of the pull to assist yourself up.

6. This can also be practiced from sitting on the floor, such as after a fall. To practice from the floor, sit up and tuck your legs into a position to get up once the dog gives a forward pull motion.

? **Need Help?** If your dog needs a refresher on pulling forward, go back to the section on teaching forward guiding (see page 114), and adapt it to pulling in a special pull harness.

TASK 2:
PROVIDING BALANCE ON STAIRS

What Does My Dog Need to Learn? For a handler with balance issues, a properly sized dog can be trained to stand–stay and brace itself for lightly balancing the human, before going up the next step. Your dog will learn to assist you on stairs by going up one step at a time as you teach them to move slowly and with precision. This exercise requires the dog to be accustomed to leash and collar handling, including yielding to collar pressure. Practice with precision heeling work will help greatly with your success in this exercise. Once your dog has mastered controlled work on steps using a collar and leash, harness bracing can be added to provide light assistance on stairs. The person should be integrating the stair rail into the process to bear weight when possible. Do not attempt to put any weight on your dog without first considering what's safe for your dog and getting approval from an orthopedic vet.

TRY THIS

1. Start by training your dog to do stairs one at a time. This starts with collar and leash handling. You may have the harness on as you train this, but it isn't necessary at this point.

2. With your dog on your left side, start at the bottom of a staircase.

3. Keep the leash short and close to you, as you will be making precise movements as you direct your dog.

4. Lead your dog slowly forward and say "step" to indicate each time they should move their feet up a step.

5. As you move up to the next step ahead of your dog, have your dog wait before stepping up on cue.

6. Pause after each step, and praise your dog on each step, when both their front feet are on it.

7. To slow your dog's pace, pull back with light tension on the leash and collar, remembering to keep a loose leash when moving forward.

8. Once you begin adding harness bracing, make sure you only apply light downward pressure to your dog when they're stopped and standing still with all four feet even and in the right position.

9. When going down stairs, teach your dog to stop and wait on the stair behind you as you step forward.

? **Need Help?** Assistance on stairs can be tricky to teach on your own. It's worthwhile to consult a trainer who specializes in mobility assistance dogs in order to make sure you're training safely.

TASK 3:
BRACING AN UNSTABLE HANDLER

What Does My Dog Need to Learn? Dizziness can be a symptom of many conditions, as well as being the side effect of some medications. Using a specially fitted harness, the dog learns to stand-stay in a rigid position and steady the handler during episodes. Bracing is never used when a dog is in motion. Before teaching bracing, the dog must know a stand position and a stay.

TRY THIS

1. A specialty bracing harness is needed, as the handler will apply light downward pressure on a rigid harness handle.

2. The height of the handle is key. Here's how to measure: Stand up straight and allow your hands to hang comfortably next to your sides. Make a fist with one hand as if you are gripping a handle. Then measure the distance from the ground to your hand.

3. Subtract your dog's height at the shoulders (remember, a dog must be fully grown and over two years old to do any weight bearing). For example, if your dog is 25 inches tall at the shoulders and the distance from the floor to your closed fist is 30 inches, you would need a handle height of about five inches.

4. It is not recommended to do mobility work using a rigid harness handle of more than six inches if you're planning to apply any downward pressure onto the dog.

5. To start practicing for bracing, begin by getting your dog comfortable with very light pressure while learning the right position.

6. Ask your dog to stand and stay. Make sure all four of their feet are squared off—meaning there's not one foot out of line and the dog is totally square and sturdy as they stand.

7. Run your hand over your dog's back, applying light hand pressure in a bouncing up-and-down motion as you pet your dog. Use just enough pressure as if you were gently pushing, and be extra careful on their spine and hips.

8. If your dog becomes distracted by this physical petting and light pressure, redirect them into the right position and try again.

9. When you get to their shoulders and withers (the area where the neck meets the shoulders), practice applying firm but gentle pressure just directly above their shoulders, praising them when they stay tensed up and still.

10. Teaching your dog to stay standing square while light pressure is applied to their shoulders will help get them ready to learn to brace in a harness.

 Need Help? It's best to consult with a trainer who specializes in mobility training in order to make sure you're doing everything correctly and safely.

SIX
HOW TO GET YOUR SERVICE DOG CERTIFIED

THE LAWS governing service dogs are explained in the Americans with Disabilities Act (ADA), which can be found online (see page 143), and with regard to air travel, the US Department of Transportation's Air Carrier Access Act (ACAA). These laws define the rights of handlers and define what a service dog is.

Outside of these laws, the service dog industry is largely self-regulated, and as such, anyone is free to train a service dog and there is no legal certification documentation you must obtain to "prove" your dog can perform service tasks. However, the industry has set certain standards of behavior for service dogs that aren't necessarily laid out in the laws, and there are organizations that "certify" dogs who meet certain standards. This chapter outlines options and best practices for getting your dog ready to work full-time.

136 WHAT ARE THE LEGAL REQUIREMENTS FOR A SERVICE DOG?

137 HOW TO PREPARE FOR THE PUBLIC ACCESS TEST

139 BASIC CERTIFICATION FACTS

WHAT ARE THE LEGAL REQUIREMENTS FOR A SERVICE DOG?

A dog is legally a service dog if it performs tasks that mitigate a disability or the symptoms of a disability. A disability is any physical or mental condition that substantially limits a major life activity. These dogs work in a partnership with one individual. While some service dogs perform several tasks, they only need to perform one task to legally be considered a service dog, as long as that task is directly related to the disability.

If a dog learns a task that is *not* related to a handler's disability, or if the handler does not have a disability, that action is considered a trick and does not count toward the animal's status as a service dog. Likewise, if a dog provides emotional support to someone with a disability but has not been trained to perform a specific task, it is not legally considered a service animal. For example, a dog's presence may provide comfort for someone with autism, but its presence alone is not enough to qualify the animal to be a service dog. However, if the dog is trained to "cover" a specific part of the handler's body on cue and provide deep pressure therapy (see page 86), that is a task that could qualify the animal as a service dog.

Service dogs and their handlers also have legal protections, such as public access rights, which means they can go anywhere with their handlers, even places where pets are forbidden. A service dog in training (SDiT) is the term for a dog who is still learning tasks for a handler. These animals do not have legally protected public access. However, most states have laws permitting SDiT access into public areas. Check your own state's legislation to make sure.

The ADA also requires that service dogs remain "under control" in public at all times, and various industry organizations, including the International Association of Canine Professionals (IACP) and the International Association of Assistance Dog Partners (IAADP) have provided guidance on standards of behavior that demonstrate this. These standards include that your service dog:

- Is reliably housebroken

- Has no history of aggression (growling, lunging, biting) to dogs or people

- Is not fearful or anxious in public

- Has advanced obedience training around distractions, including cues for heel, sit, stand, down, stay, come (including with leash dropped), tuck (tuck under a table or chair and lie down out of the way), leave it, focus (look at handler on cue), and place (lie and stay on a mat)

- Can load up into and out of the car safely on command

- Ignores other people, smells, food, and animals

- Is safe when approached by a child

- Does not jump, lick, or approach other people or dogs

- Does not eat off the floor

- Keeps "all four on the floor," meaning stays on the floor at all times, unless performing tasks for the handler that require otherwise. In public, service dogs should not be up on chairs, riding in shopping carts, or being fed from tables.

- Although it's not legally required, a service dog should be kept clean and well-groomed, and it's best to get young pups in the routine of grooming, including nail clipping, and body handling early. Many service dogs wear special gear, such as a vest or cape. Although it is not legally required, it often makes public access easier and alerts people to not interfere with your dog at work.

HOW TO PREPARE FOR THE PUBLIC ACCESS TEST

As we've discussed, task training is only a portion of service dog training, and the foundation of a well-behaved and functional service dog training is obedience. What good is a dog that can do useful tasks if they can't walk calmly on a leash around distractions? Most of the continual work you do as a team will be focused on obedience, socialization, and proper behavior in public. Public access tests (PATs) measure whether or not your dog has achieved the standards of behavior listed in the previous section (see page 136).

You can obedience train on your own, but enrolling in group classes with an experienced local trainer can be vital to accomplishing the high obedience standards required of a service dog. It can also serve as a controlled environment to work with your dog around distractions.

Not all classes are created equal. However, you should be discerning when picking them. Classes should focus on real-world obedience skills, and do not have to be specifically for service dogs. Look for classes held at a professional dog training facility, not a big box retail store, where employees typically don't receive rigorous training before teaching.

The class environment should also be considered. Many dogs in a small room, some with unchecked barking, pulling, and lunging, may end up being more of a stressful experience than a learning experience. For more specialized help, find a local trainer who has service dog experience. Private lessons can help solidify what you've studied and self-taught. See the Resources section (page 143) for trainer search recommendations.

Whether you start with a puppy or adult dog, socialization is a necessary part of your training plan. Puppy socialization is covered in many books and puppy training programs. Socializing an adult dog requires a thoughtful approach. Many people misunderstand the concept of socialization. It does not mean taking your dog everywhere with you or overwhelming them with new situations. It means being selective about which dogs your dog will interact and play with, not simply going to a dog park. It means allowing your dog to interact with others, but also using your obedience training to keep their behavior in check.

BEWARE OF BURNOUT

Keep in mind, when you're starting public access training, less is more. Start small. A 15-minute visit to a store, a 20-minute trip to the park. In the beginning, don't immediately take your dog everywhere with you. Start easy and monitor your dog's progress with each trip. Note in your training log each time you work in public, where you went, and any issues your dog might have. This helps track progress and work on specific things if necessary. For example, you might note that your dog showed hesitation when walking into an elevator. You may decide to plan a twice-weekly trip that will include a ride on the elevator.

REVIEW PUBLIC ACCESS TEST REQUIREMENTS

For an example of a thorough public access test, look online at Assistance Dogs International's (ADI) Public Access Certification Test (PACT) (see Resources, page 143). This test, or a similar one, gives you standard guidelines for evaluating whether or not your dog is ready to work full-time in public. It's helpful to have someone record you and your dog as you work through the test standards so you can review it yourself and see what you may need to work on. If you and your dog cover each part successfully and your dog's tasks are trained, then you are ready to work as a full-fledged service dog team.

BASIC CERTIFICATION FACTS

The ADA does not require written documentation, such as a certification, to "prove" your dog is a service dog. Instead, the industry is self-regulated, and professional organizations, such as Assistance Dogs International, set standards that they believe service dogs and handlers should strive to achieve.

Some organizations, like the IAADP, help set standards but do not offer certification programs. Some organizations offer private certification tests. Certification can seem like a gray area when it comes to service dogs, so here are a few important certification facts to keep in mind:

Businesses cannot ask you for proof of certification. Your service dog has the legal right to accompany you in public, including in businesses that generally forbid animals. A business cannot legally ask you to provide identification or paperwork to prove your dog is a service dog. They can only ask two questions: (1) Is that a service dog? and (2) What tasks is it trained to perform? In some cases, you can answer the task question while maintaining some privacy about your disability. For example, a handler might say "My service dog is trained to respond to a medical event by physically assisting me."

A business can ask you to leave if your dog demonstrates a lack of obedience skills. Though you don't need a physical certification, your service dog must still achieve high standards of behavior while working in public that are tested by certification programs. If your dog potties on the premises, shows aggression, or demonstrates that they are out of control, the business can ask you to leave.

There's no one official US service dog "certification." There are programs and organizations that provide trained service dogs or train dog and handler teams. These dogs might be referred to as "program dogs." The programs may issue their clients a certification through their individual organization, but that is a private certification. Most programs will not certify service dogs that did not go through that program's training course.

There are scam certifications out there. There are several online websites that will issue certificates registering a dog as a service animal for a fee. These online certification sites usually require no proof of training. Their websites are often designed to look official, but the certificates they sell are meaningless and carry no legal weight. Since the ADA does not require a certification, these sites are known as "scam registries." Some states and colleges offer voluntary registration of service animals. These usually offer a public purpose, such as providing tags that alert emergency workers that there is a service animal in the house.

Registries cannot be required, though, as that is a violation of the ADA.

It still may be a good idea to keep a training file. You still may run into situations where you must address an access issue or show proof of your dog's training, in which case a personal training file comes in handy. Include a doctor's letter stating that you have a disability. A doctor cannot write a letter saying your dog is a service dog, but they can recommend that a service dog would benefit your disabilities. You may also add your dog's medical records, training logs (including a log of hours spent training for public access), and video of your dog working in public. You may also choose to have outside evaluations, such as the Canine Good Citizen (CGC) test. This test is geared toward pets but demonstrates basic manners for any dog. Another option is to seek a public access test from an organization such as ADI, although this is not a certification.

RESOURCES

Americans with Disabilities Act | ada.gov

This is the homepage of the US Justice Department website that provides information about the laws protecting Americans with disabilities, including those that govern service dogs.

Service Animal FAQ | ada.gov/regs2010/service_animal_qa.html

This portion of the ADA website answers common questions about service animals. Print this out and keep a copy with you in case of access issues.

ADA Information Line | 800-514-0301 (Voice) 800-514-0383 (TTY)

These numbers provide information about the ADA to the public. You can call to get general information, request materials, file complaints, or ask to confidentially speak to a specialist about specific situations relating to the ADA.

Training Service Dogs | trainingservicedogs.com

This is Jennifer Hack's website for training resources.

AKC Club Search and Directory | webapps.akc.org/ club-search/#

This is the American Kennel Club's tool for finding local clubs related to training, services, and competition.

AKC Canine Good Citizen Program | akc.org/products-services/ training-programs/canine-good-citizen

This page provides information about the American Kennel Club's Canine Good Citizen program, which helps handler-and-dog teams master obedience skills necessary for public access.

IACP Service Dog Information and Resources | canineprofessionals .com/service-dog-information

This is the International Association of Canine Professionals' web page devoted to information about service dogs.

IAADP Training Standards for Public Access | iaadp.org/ iaadp-minimum-training-standards-for-public-access .html#sample

This is the International Association of Assistance Dog Partners' web page that outlines their minimum training standards for public access.

Assistance Dogs International | assistancedogsinternational.org

This coalition of nonprofits helps train and place service dogs. The website is full of resources, including the ADI's Public Access Certification Test (PACT).

TRAINING RESOURCES

Find an IACP Dog Trainer | canineprofessionals.com/ find-a-professional

This is the International Association of Canine Professionals' tool for finding a local, in-person dog trainer.

Leerburg | leerburg.com

This is an online dog training resource, with videos, online courses, and products.

Training Without Conflict | trainingwithoutconflict.com

This is a collection of video resources with trainer Ivan Balabanov.

Fenzi Dog Sports Academy | fenzidogsportsacademy.com

This website offers courses and resources for self-study as well as those with trainers.

BOOKS

***Dog Language: The Encyclopedia of Canine Behavior* | Roger Abrantes**

This helpful book teaches you to better understand your dog's behavior and build your canine vocabulary.

***How to Be Your Dog's Best Friend: The Classic Training Manual for Dog Owners* | Monks of New Skete**

Originally published in 1978, this revised edition of a classic manual is a touchstone publication on dog training. The Monks of New Skete are well known for breeding, raising, and training German shepherds at their monastery in New York.

***Let Dogs Be Dogs: Understanding Canine Nature and Mastering the Art of Living with Your Dog* | Monks of New Skete and Marc Goldberg**

This is the latest release by the Monks of New Skete and explains canine behavior and how you can address problem areas and strengthen bonds.

***My Smart Puppy: Fun, Effective, and Easy Puppy Training* | Brian Kilcommons**

This is a comprehensive, useful resource for puppy-specific training.

***The Other End of the Leash: Why We Do What We Do Around Dogs* | Patricia McConnell**

This interesting book explores human behavior in relation to dogs and why we behave the way we do around them.

INDEX

A

Air Carrier Access Act
  (ACAA), 135
Alarms, walking handler
  to, 106–107
Allergen detection dogs, 6
Americans with Disabilities
  Act (ADA), ix, 7, 135–136,
  139, 140–141
Assistance dogs. *See*
  Service dogs
Assistance Dogs International
  (ADI), 139

B

Bait bags, 19
Blocking, 90–92
Breed clubs, 9
Breeds, 7–8, 10
"Bring," 52–53. *See also*
  Carrying and
  retrieving tasks

C

Carrying and retrieving
  tasks, 44

"bring," 52–53
  delivering receipts from
    cashiers, 79–80
  dog bowl, 76–78
  drink from the
    fridge, 74
  fetch games, 46–47
  introducing new
    items, 54–55
  retrieving a
    dumbbell, 48–49
  "take it" and "hold it,"
    50–51
  unnoticed dropped items,
    104–105
Certification, 139–141
Choke chains, 16
Clickers, 15
Clock time cues,
  35–41
Clothing removal
  assistance, 72–73
Collars, 16
"Cover," 86–87
Crate training, xi
Crowd control, 90–92

D

Deep pressure therapy (DPT), 86–87
Diabetes alert dogs, 6
Distance proofing, 12
Distraction proofing, 12
Doors, opening and closing, 64–65
Duration proofing, 12

E

Elevation changes, alerting to, 120–121
Emotional support animals (ESAs), 4, 13
Equipment, 14–19
   putting on, 40–41
Exits, leading to, 116–117

F

Fetch games, 46–47
Finding a person by name, 100–101
Finding lost/misplaced items, 102–103
Following helpers, 118–119

G

Guide dogs, 6
Guiding tasks, 112
   alerting to steps/elevation changes, 120–121
   following helpers, 118–119
   leading forward on cue, 114–115
   leading to an exit/outside, 116–117
   seat-finding, 122–123

H

Harnesses, 18
Head halters, 18
Hearing dogs, 6
"Hold it," 50–51
House rules, 22–23
   "leave it," 26–27
   "settle," 24–25

I

International Association of Assistance Dog Partners (IAADP), 136, 139
International Association of Canine Professionals (IACP), 136

L

Laundry assistance, 70–71
Leading forward on cue, 114–115
Leashes, 17
"Leave it," 26–27
Legal requirements, 135–136
Lights, turning on and off, 66–67
"Look," 30–31

M

Marker training, 15, 22–23
Martingale collars, 16
Mats, 14
Medical alert and response dogs, 6, 83, 98. *See also* Psychiatric service dogs
   finding a person by name, 100–101

Medical alert and response
    dogs (*continued*)
    finding lost/misplaced
        items, 102–103
    retrieving unnoticed
        dropped items, 104–105
    waking handlers, 108–109
    waking handler to an alarm,
        106–107
Medication reminders, 88–89
Mobility dogs, 7, 111
Mobility tasks
    moving from sitting to
        standing, 128–129
    stability-bracing, 132–133
    stair balance, 130–131
    weight-bearing, 124–127

N

Negative markers, 23

O

Obedience training, 4, 21
"On/off the clock"
    cues, 35–36
    potty on, 38–39
    putting on equipment/
        gear, 40–41
Opening and closing tasks, 56
    doors, 64–65
    light switches, 66–67
    "paw-pushing"
        targets, 62–63
    pulling to drag
        objects, 58–59
    touching targets, 60–61
Outside, leading to, 116–117

P

"Paw-pushing" targets,
    62–63
Potty on cue, 38–39
Prong collars, 16
Proofing phase, 11–12
Psychiatric service dogs,
    7, 83–84
    blocking/crowd
        control, 90–92
    "cover"/deep pressure
        therapy (DPT), 86–87
    interrupting repetitive/
        self-harm
        behaviors, 96–97
    medication
        reminders, 88–89
    room checks, 93–95
Public access rights,
    3–4
Public access tests
    (PATs), 137–139
Public access training, 4–5,
    28, 138–139
    "look," 30–31
    "touch," 32–34
Pulling, 58–59
Puppies, x–xii

R

Repetitive behaviors,
    interrupting, 96–97
Rescues, 9
Retrieving. *See* "Bring";
    Carrying and
    retrieving tasks
Room checks, 93–95

S

Seat-finding, 122–123
Seizure alert dogs, 6
Self-harm behaviors,
    interrupting, 96–97
Service dog prospects, viii–ix
Service dogs
    breeds, 7–8, 10
    certification, 139–141
    equipment, 14–19
    history of, viii
    legal requirements,
        135–136
    types of, 5–7
Service dogs in training
    (SDiT), 5, 136
"Settle," 24–25
Shaping, 44
Shelters, 9
Sitting to standing, 128–129
Socialization, xi, 138
Stability-bracing, 132–133
Stair balance, 130–131
Steps, alerting to, 120–121

T

"Take it," 50–51
Task training, 5, 43. *See also*
    specific tasks
Teaching phase, 11–12
Therapy dogs, 4
"Three Ds," 12
"Touch," 32–34
Training considerations,
    11–12, 14, 22–23
Treat bags/pouches, 19

V

Vests, 19

W

Waking handlers, 108–109
Weight-bearing mobility
    tasks, 124–127

ACKNOWLEDGMENTS

I would like to thank the publisher and hardworking editors for this project. I would also like to thank my family and friends, including my dad, who has always been supportive of my unique career with animals. Training dogs has led me to meet many amazing people over the past 15 years. My colleagues in the dog training world have been invaluable. I have the utmost respect for those dog professionals who are raising the standards in training and promoting real results. Thank you for freely sharing your years of wisdom with others. I am grateful to my clients, whose hard work and successes make me proud. I'm honored to be entrusted by all of you and help you on your journeys. My hope is that the concepts in this book will help inspire people to learn how to train their own dog to a high level. Learning never ends; it's a continual process to be better than we were yesterday.

ABOUT THE AUTHOR

JENNIFER HACK is a professional dog trainer, behavior specialist, and experienced dog expert. Her knowledge and results-based methods have helped thousands of dogs and their owners live a more harmonious life. In addition to Jennifer's understanding of dog psychology and behavioral science, her natural ability with animals has led her to work in many venues. She has trained and handled every type of dog, from raising puppies to working with difficult aggressive dogs. Training service dogs has been especially rewarding work. Jennifer enjoys spending time with her own personal dogs and considers them wonderful teachers. She values the purposes dogs serve in our lives. Learn more about Jennifer at TrainingServiceDogs.com.